ASSERTIVE BLACK... PUZZLED WHITE

by Donald K. Cheek, Ph.D.

Foreword by Kenneth Clark, Ph.D.

IMPACT PUBLISHERS, INC.
Post Office Box 1094
San Luis Obispo, California 93406

First Edition, November, 1976
Second Printing, April 1977

Copyright ©1976
by Donald K. Cheek

International Standard Book Number   0-915166-33-X (paper)
                                       0-915166-32-1 (cloth)

Library of Congress Catalog Card Number   76-42867

Published by IMPACT PUBLISHERS, INC.
Post Office Box 1094
San Luis Obispo, California 93406

Cover Design by Sharon Wood.

Printed in the United States of America

Dedication

To the girl next door in Harlem who later agreed to live with me anywhere — forever.

ACKNOWLEDGEMENTS

Like any human endeavor or accomplishment, a book is the result of many people. While it is impossible to mention everyone to whom I feel indebted, there are those to whom special thanks are due:

to the Atascadero State Hospital Black Project and their leaders, who gave me a true feeling for being an assertive and valuable black therapist;

to Bob Kleiner who helped me open the door to scholarship;

to Bob Alberti and Mike Emmons for making me an offer I couldn't refuse;

to Lach MacDonald for his assistance and advice in preparing the manuscript;

to Nancy Muir for her encouragement and typing skills;

to my colleagues in the California Counselors Minority Task Force for their multi-cultural support and validation of my sanity;

to my dedicated and loving research assistant Calista Cheek for her critical reactions, unfailing enthusiasm, and reminders to be brave enough and assertive enough to write about the Black Experience like it really is.

D.K.C.

CONTENTS

Foreword, Kenneth B. Clark, Ph.D. vii

I. What Is This Book About? 1
   Wherein you and I discuss this book, why it was written, some of my frustration with white approaches to meeting black needs and how the book attempts to deal with overcoming that problem.

II. Black Strokes and White Folks 13
   Black Tradition Looks at White Therapy ... The Assertive Training Approach ... Passiveness: A Strategy for Racism ... A Black Definition ... Modifying Conventional Therapy ... Assertive Behavior – Relevance for Blacks ... How To Use This Book.

III. A Foundation for the Black Perspective 23
   Frame of Reference ... A Personal Note ... Black Issues and Answers ... Black and White Therapists ... Professional Blacks View Whites ... Jim Crow and Its Effect on Therapy ... Black Styles – 10 Characteristics ... White Skills and Black Clients.

IV. Assertive Behavior and Black Lifestyles 43
   The Black Experience ... New Requirements for Old Problems ... Changing to Assertiveness – First Five Steps ... Why a White Approach Can Fail.

V. Black Rappin and Cappin 51
   Black Message – Mode and Style ... Black-White Language Comparison ... Who is the Target? ... Comparison of Black-White and Black-Black Interaction ... Assertive Black Messages ... Message Matching ... Will the Assertive Message Fit? ... The Intention and the Message – A Didactic Approach.

VI. Techniques from a Black Perspective 73
   Tools for Assertive Training ... The Assertive Inventory ... The Survival Ladder ... A Black-White Language Questionnaire ... The "Before You Work With Blacks" Test ... A Group Awareness Profile (GAP Test).

VII. Guiding the Black Client to Effective Assertion 87

VIII. Assertive Guidelines from a Black Perspective 91
   A Black Assertive Training Program ... Structure of a Black Assertive Behavior Training Program ... Short Cut Assertive Behavior Training ... Let's Put It Into Action – A Step-by-Step Guide for a Black A-T Group ... Teaching Black Assertion.

IX. Lifting the Veil of Color 119

Bibliography 125

Appendix I 129

Appendix II 132

FOREWORD

In 1965 in my introduction to *Dark Ghetto*, I wrote that a respected friend accused me of not permitting "the facts to interfere with the truth." This accusation, which I have never denied, was made before computers became the dominant tool of many highly publicized social scientists. In a recent joint seminar at the City College of the City University of New York, my friend Gunnar Myrdal and I repeatedly insisted to our students that no amount of quantification of data could successfully disguise the fact that the social sciences are rooted in human values. Moral and ethical concerns can not be avoided in an objective study of human interaction. Any attempt to define social science objectivity in terms of a "balanced view" which seeks to evade or deny moral and human truths is transparent and neither objective or scientific.

In this book, my friend, Don Cheek, moves beyond a narrow view of quantifiable facts to the emotional content of being black in this society. He not only points out the questionable assumptions and neglected multi-cultural analysis of white professionals in the Mental Health field but he also offers a new approach based on the truth of the psychological totality of the Black Experience in an American society permeated with subtle and flagrant forms of racism. He draws on his own observations and background, being born and raised in the ghetto of Harlem, New York. He analyzes the behavior around himself as a sensitive social scientist, a systematic researcher and an astute observer of the frailties of mankind.

This book deals with complex racial and social psychological issues in a direct, forceful and straightforward manner. Dr. Cheek does not equivocate in his evaluation of white oriented theories and clinicians. He brings us back to basic human considerations in a penetrating examination of the meaning of being black in this society. As a result, he confronts his colleagues in the social science and Mental Health fields with some relevant issues and some profound ethical questions.

The contents of this work deftly reveal the sophisticated forms of racism contained in the assumptions and practices of the social sciences and helping professions. This book clearly presents a case that shows why a large segment of our society is not receiving adequate treatment or therapy. It shows how inadequate many ideas about mental health are if the cultural and social psychological background of the client is ignored and not considered of value. Thus, the book's reference to the provocative concept of "culturally deprived whites."

Dr. Cheek proposes a test for those who are interested in treating and working with black clients. He particularly emphasizes the psycho-historical effects of the Jim Crow period of our society and points out how the implications of such an experience are more or less ignored in the training of current or future therapists and members of the helping professions. This book, indeed, gives us all a great deal to consider when we evaluate the meaning and relevance of a white dominated social and behavioral science for those members of society who have had non-white experiences. The hope within this book is its belief that if we improve the treatment, therapy and mental health services rendered to black clients, we will not only benefit all Americans, but we will also be well on our way toward remedying American racism.

Kenneth B. Clark

CHAPTER I

What Is This Book About?

Why is there need for a book on assertiveness from a black viewpoint? How does this book really differ from other books written on assertive behavior? What are some of the basic points that I will be attempting to get across to you, the reader? Coming from an oral tradition, I think these and other pertinent questions can best be handled by an informal rap with you. Imagine you and I getting together to seriously discuss assertive behavior as it pertains to black people. You come to my home and we sit in the front room with a view of hillsides covered with toyon shrubs and wild grass. You relax with a glass of Cribari Vin Rosé and pick up on sounds of Quincy Jones playing in the background. We both kick back and start to rap.

Me: O.K., What would you like to know?

You: As simple as possible, what does your book try to say?

Me: Man, life's not simple. The black experience is not simple. In fact, that's just the point. I really started writing because I knew people (especially whites) didn't want to listen to anything complex. We create a big-ass racial mess in this society and then have nerve enough to ask for simple answers.

You: Why are you getting upset?

Me: (I sit back pause and smile and take a deep breath). I'm not really upset — just emotional and maybe somewhat frustrated. And let me say this — just because I use certain words differently from you — maybe words that you were taught not to use — that doesn't mean that I'm mad or upset — just that I am freely expressing myself — Is that cool with you?

You: (Hesitatingly) Yeah, that's O.K.

Me: Alright — let's take it from the top. There are a large number of black people who could be helped to improve their social and personal functioning. They need to be guided by an approach that is not just meant for white people or has a white orientation. Black clients or patients, or let's just say black people trying to improve on the way they live, need to have an approach that they can relate to — an approach that takes into consideration the things that they share with whites along with the things that make them different from whites. And in many important ways they are different — they have a unique lifestyle that has been talked about and written about — call it the American Dilemma or the Mark of Oppression or maybe what John O. Killens calls the Black Man's Burden.

You: Can I interrupt?

Me: Sure, sure.

You: Why do you keep stressing this difference between blacks and whites?

Me: I am really not interested in stressing it; I am interested in placing the problem in a proper perspective. Well, maybe that sounds kinda corny. The truth is that a lot of white people, therapists, clinicians, professionals and all that, you know, so-called educated whites — well, they just don't want to hear it either.

    I talk about racial differences because many blacks and particularly whites are exposed to education and training that covers up the shit of racial oppression in this society.

    I talk about racial differences because black people are frequently exposed to white helpers who are puzzled — most of them, in fact, are basically ignorant (sometimes arrogantly so) and incompetent when it comes to treating, guiding or being therapeutically helpful to blacks.

    I talk about racial differences because they exist, but are not studied, examined, analyzed and discussed by the professionals who claim they want to work with or help black clients. Most white people don't know a damn thing about the psychology of the black experience — do you?

You: I have gone to school with many blacks and I have some blacks whom I would consider my friends. We get along quite well and I don't think they are dishonest with me.

Me: That may be true, but the point is that I feel those who are in responsible helping positions and who provide professional service to black persons, should be aware of how impoverished their training has been (along with their formal education) as it pertains to the Black Experience. Just look at all the things that happened in this country that have ramifications for how blacks see themselves and how they see whites — slavery, lynching, Jim Crow laws, miscegenation, passing, religion, matriarchy, ghetto living, and disenfranchisement — along with all the routine segregation and discrimination and the constant exposure to white symbols of beauty and goodness.

You: You sound bitter.

Me: In a way, yes. I have five black children that go to so-called good schools and they do nothing but study white people. Their white school mates never study black people in a normal, academic, routine way — they must wait for brotherhood week or Black History week or some old bullshit like that.

You: Why do you call it bullshit; isn't that type of racial recognition worthwhile?

Me: It's a band-aid on cancer. Black people have been part of this society from the very beginning. There shouldn't be the need for a special week to discuss their contributions — like Carver and the peanut.

You: You lost me.

Me: Just a joke — seems like the only thing white teachers seem to remember to discuss is George Washington Carver and his research with the peanut — dig that name, too.

You: I still don't get your point.

Me: Have you ever read the novels of Charles Chestnutt or James Weldon Johnson — the short stories of Langston Hughes and Jean Tommer — or the poetry of Paul Lawrence Dunbar, Claude McKay or Countee Cullen — or say the essays of Horace Cayton, Ira Reid or Carter G. Woodson?

You: I've heard of Langston Hughes.

Me: Good for you. The point is that all of those mentioned are black writers and their names should appear on any school's reading list — but they don't.

You: Umm (quietly staring at me).

Me: You see, you asked me why I stress the differences between blacks and whites. Because of social conditions (better known as racism) those differences *do* exist. You expose a group of people to all those things that I mentioned — segregated armies, segregated schools, years of being told to sit in back of buses, to drink from separate water fountains, watching caricatures of yourself in movies, and being referred to as *nigger, boy, coon* and *spade* – you take the years of being told that white is right, of being told your hair is bad, of hearing about uppity niggers being lynched, of experiencing white law and all white juries — you take all that shit as part of your roots and and part of the fears of black parents and grandparents and you have a group of people who are different in many ways from those who were not the targets of such action — I call those white people.

Then you have theories of behavior developed by whites who don't know a damn thing about this black lifestyle. You get Sigmund Freud, and Lewin and Skinner, Rogers, Jung and what all. Well, you get these "white oriented" theories — those dudes have never been in any black ghettoes — except driving by quickly — and you get ignorance compounding ignorance as far as blacks are concerned.

You: You lost me a little with that last point.

Me: What I'm saying is this: you first have theoretical and therapeutic ideas that have little relevance for blacks. Then you get professionals who are trained and educated with little, if any, exposure to the meaning of the black experience as it relates to the behavior of black clients. And yet these are the people who apply the theories.

You: I follow you now.

Me: This is why I sum up the general reaction of whites as being puzzled. Based on the limited information most whites have about blacks, they find it difficult to make sense out of their behavior.

You: Isn't it difficult to make a statement about what all or most whites feel?

Me: Interesting point. Blacks have been collecting and sharing information about whites in this country for over three hundred years. Blacks have worked in their kitchens, cleaned their homes, raised white children, listened to their domestic problems and slept with frustrated masters and mistresses — if there is anything a black is an expert on, it is white people — if for no other reason than survival.

You: I see.

Me: So, when it comes to black behavior, you could say that some blacks see whites as curious, stupid, unaware, ignorant or oblivious. But on a feeling level, blacks get the underlying message behind the question which most characterizes a white reaction when it is asked, "What do they want?" This is the traditional white response to ghetto burning, demonstrations, riots and black demands. Blacks see whites as puzzled by the rebellious behavior of "darkies" who were supposed to be happy — puzzled by blacks like Cassius Clay, Leroi Jones and Lew Alcindor who changed their slave names — puzzled by the emphasis on black studies (as if white studies was not good enough); by the insistence that black holidays and black national heroes be recognized. It is again anticipated that as blacks leave aggressiveness and become assertive — when blacks speak up, talk back and "don't remember their place," there will be cause for whites to wonder "What do they want?" Whites will face assertive blacks and be obviously or secretly puzzled.

You: Umm (intensely staring at me).

Me: So what do you have — a bunch of well-meaning (let's be optimistic) puzzled white folks, taking theories meant for white folks (excuse me — they say it pertains to the generic behavior of all people) and applying these theories to black folks about whom they know very little except what might be picked up from black friends, mass media or maybe sleeping with a black lover.

You: I see your point.

Me: This is why in my book I talk about the psycho-historical implications of the past, the Jim Crow Halo Effect and propose a test for therapists who desire to work with blacks.

You: But —

Me: Let me say this — I also know that there are some blacks who may not be able to pass my test for therapist. You see, our white brainwashing education is a bitch — it doesn't tell whites about blacks, but what is even more nasty, it doesn't tell blacks about themselves either. A lot of people wondered what the cry for Black Studies was all about — well, it may have died down but the need is just as crucial. I have occasion to talk with young people trained at the Masters and Ph.D. level who know nothing about miscegenation, Jim Crow laws or the phenomenon of passing and "the dozens" — yet they want to help black clients along with the

others. Man — these white folks are culturally deprived and so are
the people who are teaching them.

You: Well, back to the book —

Me: Screw the book — you need to understand what I'm saying! The
lives of many black people are in the hands of whites, and maybe
some blacks, who are incompetent when it comes to really
deeply picking up on where that black person is coming from.
These are whites and blacks too (if the shoe fits, wear it) who are
wrapped up in all the theoretical bullshit that is part of the western
and European view of behavior. And I include myself. Baby, it is
hard to extricate yourself from all that jargon and shit. But yet, we
also can't throw out the baby with the bathwater. There are some
basic ideas that can be modified and made of value to skin-color-
stigmatized people. I use that phrase because Erving Goffman is a
good example of a scholar that developed a meaningful
theoretical position that has relevance for blacks — the concept of
stigma.

You: So, everything white or Western or European is not bad?

Me: No, not bad, just white oriented or biased — some more than
others. By the way, I'm sorry I cut you off earlier — I guess I get
carried away with the need to explain the frustration of — well,
look at this, it's an article by Herbert Hill, national labor director
for the NAACP — "Blacks Still Lag in Jobs, Income." Just check
out some of these facts — "After the gains of the civil rights
movement of the 1960's, black income peaked in 1969-1970 at
61% of the income earned by whites. Since then, there has been a
steady decline. In 1971 black family income fell to 60%: in 1972
to 59%; in 1973-74 to 58%; and in 1975 to 56% ...At the
beginning of 1976 the official employment rate in the nation was
7.6% for whites; 14.1% for blacks ...there is a systematic
undercount which especially distorts the official rate of
unemployment among nonwhite workers ...The more accurate
unemployment figure would be 13.6% for whites; 25.5% for
blacks." The article goes on to say — are you *listening* to this?

You: Yes, I'm listening.

Me: The article goes on to say "Data from the 25 major areas of black
urban population show that in some communities black

unemployment is in excess of 30%, while black teenage unemployment is close to 50%. In 1933 the national unemployment rate was 24.9%, the highest official recorded unemployment rate in the history of the United States. The unemployment rate among black workers in many inner city areas now exceeds the general rate of unemployment for the entire nation during the Great Depression of the 1930's." (See Hill, 1970, in Bibliography.) Now I think that's some heavy shit — in this society if you don't have some coins, you are dead.

You: (Silently nod your head).

Me: I guess those are the kinds of things I have in mind when I talk about the black experience — when I stress the difference between blacks and whites.

You: But there are poor whites, too.

Me: Yeah, there are poor whites and I'm sure you may eventually mention the plight of women too — white women. But you see, white skin has been the traditional passport into the opportunity structure of this country. As for white women we have more female millionaires in this country than males. White women have not been subjected to systematic lynching, allowed to fight for this country but not to vote in it, segregated in all social activities from the cradle to the grave, with the display of degrading public signs providing evidence of their inferiority.

You: I think I could argue that point with you.

Me: Yes, that's another issue. I'll let the sisters preach on that one. Let me concentrate on the black perspective.

You: Can you come back to your book?

Me: Don't worry, I haven't forgotten. My book basically aims to do three things — first, take a look at a worthwhile approach (assertive training); second, suggest changes to make it of value to blacks; and third, provide black oriented information to those (black or white) who may wish to use assertive training with blacks.

You: How does your approach to assertive training differ from others?

Me: Glad you asked me that. In reading most of the popular works on assertive training — (or as some like to call it, assertiveness training, or assertion training, or assertive behavior training) I find at least four areas that keep the material from really being of value to blacks:

First, the interracial implications of assertiveness are ignored. This is exemplified by what I call the "somebody syndrome" — questions and examples about somebody with no consideration for the possibility of a white asserter and a black assertee and vice versa.

Second, the stress on appropriateness of behavior with no mention that cultural background may affect what a person considers appropriate.

Third, a social class bias in that the examples are very middle class or above — problems about swimming pools and mothers being confused about child-rearing practices because of reading Spock, Gesell or Patterson. But nowhere any racial examples.

You: For example?

Me: Several current popular books about assertiveness. Most black parents are not that hip on Spock, Gesell or Patterson.

But let me get on one author's case, a writer by the name of Fensterheim. He really would put black folks into a bind because on one hand he says "overassertiveness is often aggression and always inappropriate" on page 46, but on page 49 he says, "you have the right to maintain your dignity by being properly assertive — even if it hurts someone else — as long as your motive is assertive, not aggressive."

Well, my *fourth* point is that most authors are not clear about *intent* while, for black clients *intent* is *very* important.

You: I'm not sure I understand why each point is so important for assertive training with blacks?

Me: Look. Let's take point one as an example — the interracial implications. All of the popular assertive training books talk about doing things like asking for a date and introducing yourself to a stranger, right?

You: Right.

Me: Well, none of them say anything about a black dude being assertive and asking a white chick for a date or what about some assertive white dude introducing himself to a tough black fox — in Watts or Harlem. You dig where I'm coming from?

You: I'm beginning to get the picture. In other words there are other kinds of problems to be dealt with when — to use your words — the asserter is white or black and the assertee is of the opposite race.

Me: Right on. This is why I talk about the communicator and the target person. In reading the current books on assertiveness, you can just see from the examples cited and language used that both the communicator and target person share the same skin color — white. Most of the authors, I believe, would freely admit this. That's like the flesh-colored band aid.

You: The flesh colored band aid?

Me: Yeah — what color is the flesh-colored band aid?

You: Pink — oh, I see what you mean.

Me: Right on, baby. The man making flesh-colored band aids didn't consider my color — of if he did obviously he decided it wasn't that important.

You: That's an interesting point.

Me: So you see, assertive training has been developed like the flesh colored band aid — and what I'm trying to do is give it a little color — yeah, I guess it's just that simple. Come to think about it, I guess that's the most simple way of saying what my book is about . . . to give assertive training some *color!*

You: Why assertive training?

Me: You know, that's interesting. The way I see assertive training, *it is really of more value to blacks than to whites.* Look around at this society and who needs the most help in being accepted for their honest, open and direct expression? Blacks. You see, assertive training is ready made for blacks. Listen to this passage, "The person who fails to stand up for his rights has little freedom, feels uncomfortable and afraid, and, in his hunger for freedom, may sometimes turn 'vicious' with inappropriate outbursts. For such people, assertiveness training consists of teaching them to know their legitimate rights, how to stand up for them and prevent them from being usurped."

You: Who said that?

Me: Fensterheim, on page 25 of his book *Don't Say Yes When You Want to Say No* — a very heavy dude. You see what I mean —

ready made. He even gets into self-esteem — like the more you stand up for yourself and act in a manner you respect, the higher will be your self-esteem.

You: Then what are you so critical about?

Me: (Taking a deep breath). Because that dude, like the rest writing about assertiveness, doesn't realize the implications of what he is saying when applied to black people.

You: Please go slow, I'm trying to follow you.

Me: Look — when all of these assertive behavior authors do their writing, who do you think they have in mind — I mean what race?

You: Whites?

Me: Yeah, that's right, whites. Now, when they talk about applying an assertive approach to real life, whose life are they thinking about and what examples do they use?

You: Well — I guess you would say a white lifestyle.

Me: Right, that's it — they are thinking about themselves — white. The majority of patients they see are what? — white; and what's the lifestyle they know best? — a white lifestyle. And that's cool, baby. I got no quarrel with that. But shit, man, don't make believe that it's relevant to blacks — I mean the idea may be good, but the authors never break it down to apply to black lifestyles, black patients and black examples.

You: I'm beginning to see what you mean.

Me: I mean go back to that dude, Fensterheim — don't you think black folks have tried to stand up for their rights — don't you think they have tried to be honest, open and direct and maintain their dignity?

You: Yes.

Me: You are wrong. That's just the point. A black person has got to know when to be assertive and when to kiss ass.

You: But so does everybody.

Me: I mean it in terms of survival baby — survival — I mean whether or not the man even lets you live. Ain't that many whites who got to worry about being killed because they want to be assertive enough to vote.

You: But —

Me: Hold on — you see the authors on assertiveness have not

sufficiently considered the social conditions in which blacks live — and have lived. That blind spot in many ways alters or changes the manner that assertiveness is applied. Listen, man — a black had better be cool reading a white-oriented book on assertiveness, lest he forget about "white citizens councils" and the KKK.

You: Aren't those extreme situations?

Me: Man — check out the attitudes of good Catholics in South Boston — just the other night NBC did a little thing on open housing and showed films of a brother Ezra Buckner in Forest Park near Chicago, getting his home burned up, for what — for being assertive enough to move into the neighborhood of his choice. And like I say — you start to being assertive and dating white chicks or white dudes or whatever in the wrong place in front of the wrong people and that may be your ass.

You: But — well, I guess you just can't change some people.

Me: Look — I'm not trying to blow you away — I'm just trying to say that the current assertive authors have a great approach — it is an approach that can really aid black folks, in fact they need it — but at the time *these authors are unable to translate assertive training into the examples, language and cautions that fit the realities of a black lifestyle.* When I see assertive black folks, I think of black youth knowing how to promote themselves for better jobs. I think of black parents in an exploitive environment — dealing assertively with landlords, school teachers, social workers and police and people like that.

You: Well, isn't that what assertive books teach?

Me: Generally speaking, yes, but the flesh colored band aid is still there. The black perspective deals with assertive language and styles that flow out of the black community — this defines what is appropriate for some occasions. You see, most blacks must live in two worlds — we must exist with whites and live with blacks.

Dig this: Black patients at Atascadero State Hospital are exposed to "white oriented" social skills classes and all that shit — well, that might be cool if only it was recognized that most of those black dudes must return to a black community where the social skill is how to say, "Look, my man — I said don't mess with me — you dig, mothafucka?" At times *that* is survival language in the black community. Yet there are even some therapy teams that want to change the way a black patient walks, his tone of voice and the way he raps — which is again taking away from his survival repertoire.

I have come to the conclusion that these "white oriented" skills are necessary — they help a minority person to survive in a white dominated society. But both skills should be equally valued and developed. It's almost like Spanish and English for Latins. English should be definitely learned but not by putting down Spanish or the value of being bilingual.

You: So this is what your book does?

Me: Yes — that's why I use the term didactic assertive training. I feel it's necessary for the communicator or asserter to be aware of who the target person is and to develop the assertive message accordingly. Sometimes a black person has a white target, sometimes a black target and sometimes a marginal or dual oriented target — one who is equally at home with white and black communication styles. If the training is going to be relevant, all the cautions and examples consistent with these different target persons should be discussed.

You: Can a white person teach black patients — I mean can a white professional helper conduct assertive training for blacks?

Me: Generally speaking, no — first they have to read my book. (laughter). No — I'm just joking — second thought, I'm not. It would be very difficult for the average culturally-deprived, *puzzled* white to conduct assertive training for blacks — but check out my "Before You Work With Blacks" test. As you can see it means being pretty familiar and comfortable with black lifestyles. Of course, I'm talking about the ideal and I'm well aware that there are sisters and brothers with the right skin color who may not be very capable of answering the questions I raise. But I see my book as a beginning in that direction — in the direction of getting competent helpers, black or white, to assist blacks to become assertive instead of "aggressive or passive."

You: I'd like a little more wine.

Me: Think I'll join you.

CHAPTER II

Black Strokes and White Folks

> "I want you to overcome 'em with yeses, undermine 'em with grins, agree 'em to death and destruction, let 'em swoller you till they vomit or bust wide open."
> — Ralph Ellison
> *Invisible Man*

BLACK TRADITION LOOKS AT WHITE THERAPY

These last words of a dying old man to his black grandchildren capture the dilemma. It's the frustration of dealing with the many subtle dimensions that exist when a person is black in this society. It's the fear of not being able to assist the reader in understanding the behavioral ramifications of living the black experience. It's the complexity of taking that old man's warning as it reflects the black reality of past and present — putting it together with up-to-date ideas about behavior — while not losing sight of the validity and limits of both positions. It's the question of how one combines the pragmatic lessons learned from the traditional black experience with the trusting hope of becoming the more fully enriched person as advocated by the new therapeutic approaches. It's the black grandfather versus the white social scientist.

Being a social psychologist and having my roots in the black community I ponder both sides. My loyalties are automatic. I look at all white ideologies with suspicion (that's my grandfather's side). But I also seek a deeper knowledge of the behavior of all men as it is conditioned by person-to-person relationships in a social context. I believe we can learn enough about people to suggest that there are some better ways of acting or relating that are more productive for all concerned. But principles of behavior that have been accumulated in the body of knowledge of social science — those principles from which spring theories of personality, therapy, and counseling — are not readily applicable to many representatives of the black community except with a good deal of modification and translation. It is from this standpoint — the translation needed — that I discuss the assertive training approach. This is the position from which I will evaluate the development and relevance of assertive behavior for blacks.

THE ASSERTIVE TRAINING APPROACH

Before continuing we need to take a brief look at the basic ideas contained in the assertive training approach. Just a look at the titles of some of the current books on assertive behavior can give the reader the feeling for what it is all about — *Your Perfect Right; I Can If I Want To; Stand Up, Speak Out, Talk Back; The Assertive Woman; Don't Say Yes When You Want To Say No.* These authors are dealing with the assertive training theme of helping a person to please himself or herself instead of always trying to please others — they attempt to enable individuals to change their actions so that they can counter the neurotic fears which keep them from being open, honest and direct in their relationships. Assertive behavior training attempts to show you how to stand up for your rights, say *no* when you want to say *no* and *yes* when you want to say *yes*, to openly express positive feelings, to judge your own behavior and not to be manipulated by others, to ask favors and make requests, to deal with criticism and generally to direct your own life. This approach seeks to enhance your emotional freedom and to increase your feelings of self respect.

Assertive behavior training teaches skills, actions, words, phrases and ideas that make you more capable of relating to people in ways that meet your own needs. The techniques of role playing, social modeling, behavior assignments, video taping and self observation are all used. In addition, training includes detailed analysis of the assertive act with attention given to eye contact, body posture, gestures, facial expressions, voice tone, inflection, and volume, along with the timing and content of spontaneous expression.

Several theoreticians — Andrew Salter, Joseph Wolpe, Arnold Lazarus, Robert Alberti, and Michael Emmons — are usually credited with developing the major concepts employed in assertive training. Andrew Salter is recognized as the first therapist to deal systematically with assertiveness, although using somewhat a different term. In his 1949 book, *Conditioned Reflex Therapy,* he presented the concept of "excitatory behavior," and discussed the importance of "feeling talk" — an uninhibited direct expression of feelings. Similarly, Wolpe (1969), first to use the term "assertive training," refers to getting rid of inhibiting feelings as "deconditioning of unadaptive anxiety habits of response to people with whom the patient interacts." The whole idea is to teach individuals to behave in such a way as to deal with or control their fears, anxieties and inhibitions which prevent them from expressing their real feelings. This approach has been found to be helpful in enabling people to get rid of their uptight feelings which prevent them from really doing and saying what they want. As Wolpe says, "Assertive behavior is defined as the proper expression of any emotion other than anxiety towards another person."

Lazarus (1971), taking a somewhat different position, has warned us that "many people associate assertive training with oneupmanship and other deceptive games and ploys which Wolpe includes under this heading and which have no place in the forthright and honest expression of one's basic feelings." Thus Lazarus makes a point of saying that for him " . . .the term assertive behavior will denote only that aspect of emotional freedom that concerns standing up for one's rights." Lazarus feels that there are other areas of expression which are not included in the concept of assertiveness. He contrasts assertiveness with the idea of "emotional freedom" which would include the subtleties of love and affection, empathy and compassion, admiration and appreciation, curiosity and interest, as well as anger, pain, remorse, skepticism, fear, and sadness. Lazarus points out that training in "emotional freedom" implies the recognition and appro-priate expression of each and every affective state. It should be noted, however, that this pioneer in assertive training gives no recognition to the possibility that "appropriate expression" may be directly related to one's culture, social class or ethnicity, and thus, like the others who have written on the topic, does not deal with the racial implications of assertiveness.

Although the goals of assertive behavior training are geared to the freedom of people to express themselves, it must be recognized that other modes of expression are also available. How a person may develop assertive responses for situations which had in the past encouraged aggressive or non-assertive behavior is an area discussed by my colleagues Robert Alberti and Michael Emmons. In their book, *Your Perfect Right,* they provide a clear distinction between behavior that is *assertive* and behavior that is *aggressive* or *non-assertive.* In a non-assertive response, the person is typically denying self and is inhibited from expressing his or her actual feelings ... aggressive behavior commonly results in a "put-down" of the recipient. The person's rights have been denied, and he or she feels hurt, defensive, and humiliated. Assertive behavior is self-enhancing for that person, and an honest expression of his or her feelings.

In using the Alberti-Emmons conceptual distinction as a point of departure, I discuss *aggressive* and *assertive* behavior from a black perspective. However, in contrast to their terminology, I use the term *passive* instead of *non-assertive*. Considering the oppressive conditions historically faced by blacks and one of the survival techniques frequently used — which was to appear to ignore a situation — I feel that *passive* is a more "culturally" consistent term than *non-assertive*. "Non" is a prefix meaning *not*; therefore non-assertive would indicate that there is an absence of assertiveness. The strategy of blacks facing hostile whites was to give the appearance of being submissive and of offering no resistance. The goal of those blacks interested in surviving was to put on an act for the white man— to act like you were passive even though you felt aggressive or assertive. This passive act began to have special meaning to blacks since frequently there was no choice involved — one had to ignore insults and abuse or risk the wrath of whites. Passiveness grew to have a special meaning in the Black Experience. I therefore use the term *passive* as other authors use *non-assertive*.

PASSIVENESS: A STRATEGY FOR RACISM

The modification of different approaches that I earlier spoke about are necessary because my white colleagues tend to be unaware of the deep implications of the black grandfather's warning. For purposes of survival, blacks learned early *not* to be assertive — *not* to be honest, *not* to exercise their own rights, or stand up for themselves. Under the debilitating color-conscious system of this society, blacks were (and still are) rewarded for telling whites what they wanted to hear. And so behavior which allowed blacks to deal with the insanity of racism by placating and neutralizing the white oppressor took the form of "overcome 'em with yeses, undermine 'em with grins."

Despite the militancy of many of today's blacks, that style born of survival is still seen. It is currently put into the slang expression, "shine 'em on," but the function is still the same — don't let the white man know what you really feel and think. This passive form of behavior has been a traditional mask for hostility, anger and aggression. For many blacks, such behavior defined as passive by white standards, is viewed as aggressive by black standards. The non-verbal communication contained in one's cutting eyes, sucking one's teeth, looking away from the speaker or silently staring at the speaker just begin to touch on the many mannerisms and silent ways an oppressed people can express their contempt in terms of in-group language.

With every label, such as *aggressive*, *assertive*, *non-assertive* or *passive* there are behaviors or observable activities that are usually agreed upon as being consistent with the definition. We agree upon what the behavior means to the extent that we share cultural attitudes and understandings. A loud belch during dinner may be a breach of etiquette in American society while it stands as a compliment in another culture. Different definitions for the same behavior. So the playing of music in a loud manner, the wearing of braided corn-rows or the particular style of walk may be *assertive* behavior by some definitions and *aggressive* or *passive* by others.

With these different standards in mind the concept of assertiveness as applied to whites has been translated and modified to the realities of the black experience before we can say the term has equal meaning to both.

A BLACK DEFINITION

The legal and social separation of blacks and whites in this society has created certain realities that conventional assertive training does not deal with. As mentioned earlier, none of the books on assertive training discuss interracial assertiveness. Because of contrasting values and lifestyles between many blacks and whites there are also different "definitions of the situation." Ideas about "appropriate" behavior, standing up for rights and freely expressing feelings are not to be automatically adopted by blacks. Blacks have vivid memories and stories about those "blacks who didn't stay in their place." Many blacks who asserted themselves by voting have been banned from employment, blacks who have asserted themselves by relating to white women have been lynched, blacks who have asserted themselves by moving into neighborhoods of their choice have been burned out. The message of assertiveness is heard and defined differently by blacks than by whites. Even the loud strong voices of many blacks, their hair styles, manner of dress and use of slang "street talk" is not in the realm of appropriate behavior as viewed by many whites. In considering the appropriate manner to communicate feelings to a person jumping in front of him or her in line, a black could very easily say, "Hey man, why don't you get your ass out of the line" which could have no intent of "putting someone down." A white could hear this as a "put-down" and define it as aggressive—especially if the message is accompanied by a loud voice, a "militant" appearance, and a direct stare.

For blacks, then, one of the best definitions of assertiveness is an honest, open and direct verbal or non-verbal expression which *does not have the intent of putting someone down.* This definition allows for the possibility that the target person or recipient of an assertive expression may indeed be upset and hurt. My definition differs from that of Alberti and Emmons and others who contend that each person has the right to express himself "as long as he does not hurt others in the process." I maintain that because many whites are not accustomed to what might be appropriate according to the standards of the black community, there is the possibility of being hurt without this being the intention. The *intentions* of the assertive black person should be the basis for judgment, not the *responses* of the target person. I will discuss ways that the black person may be helped to "match the message" to become more effective in communication. But my basis for labeling the behavior is still the *intent of the black communicator.*

Aggressive behavior is defined as any open and direct verbal or non-verbal expression which has the intent of putting the person down. *Passiveness* is behavior that is intended to give the impression of not responding to a person or situation. Issues and examples involving these definitions will be discussed later in more detail when we consider developing assertive messages for people of various racial orientations.

MODIFYING CONVENTIONAL THERAPY

The past messages of one's tradition, the contemporary thrust of black culture and the never-changing struggle to survive in a white society fashions an intricate lifestyle that defies most, if not all, traditional and conventional forms of therapy. As counselors, therapists and other "helping agents" can attest, blacks do not respond to many "white techniques" to enhance personal growth.

Yet, there is a need that sensitive people can fill in enabling themselves and others to feel more self-satisfied (or should I say satisfied with "self"). I have found black couples unhappy in their pursuit of love and mutual companionship because one partner was making all the decisions while the other felt inhibited and hurt in "going along with the program." I have several cases in mind where I have psychologically supported a young black marital partner to stop being a doormat and become self-assertive — to the benefit of the relationship. There are specific needs that blacks share with all people with regard to interpersonal relationships.

Blacks, like everyone else, benefit from guidance in choosing more productive and satisfying ways of relating to each other — and of relating to those who are not black. To state the obvious, blacks have problems too; with each other, with parents, wives, husbands, children, neighbors, co-workers, teachers, counselors, and all those who represent the society in which one must function. And blacks, again like others, need more viable alternatives as to therapies, approaches or suggested behaviors that reflect their atypical experience in a racist society. Yes, blacks need help, but it must be help fashioned from a black perspective and from a black viewpoint. And white "helping agents" will also benefit from knowing something about therapy from a black perspective so they will be less prone to a myopic allegiance to the traditional approaches taught them in white schools, by white teachers, from theoretical assumptions standardized on white populations.

Let's look at an example of a black style which although assertive and effective, is easily misunderstood by a "culturally deprived" puzzled white counselor.

A black young lady is brought to the attention of the white high school counselor, and accused of being disorderly in the lunch room and using "improper language."

Counselor: What were you doing in the lunchroom?

Girl: Nuthin.

Counselor: Why were you brought to this office?

Girl: Ask the lady who brought me here.

Counselor: They said you were disorderly and using bad language.

Girl: I didn't do nuthin wrong.

Counselor: Could you tell me what happened?

Girl: (Silence)

Counselor: Did someone bother you?

Girl: Yeah. As usual.

Counselor: I would like to try and understand. Would you tell me about it?

Girl: No big thing — this boy asked me for some pussy. I told him to ask his momma. Then he put his hands on me and I told him, "Nigger, take your black hands off me — I'm not your momma."

Counselor: Well, that wasn't a nice thing to say.

Girl: Yes it was; he stopped botherin me.

One who is not familiar with the black communication style called "the dozens" or lacks an understanding of "survival type speech" will completely misinterpret the value of the black girl's assertiveness. If the counselor was "culturally deprived" according to black standards, he or she could be lost in knowing how to deal constructively with the young lady. Thus the puzzled white response results in no help to the student and frustration for the counselor.

ASSERTIVE BEHAVIOR — RELEVANCE FOR BLACKS

In approaching the concept of assertiveness, then, I view it as a means of facilitating black people to attain their personal goals. I perceive it as a way of freeing blacks from enslavement to a traditional "black role" and allowing them to speak out for themselves whether it be to a white or to a fellow black. I see assertive behavior from a black perspective in many ways:

- It's walking into a shop with all white barbers, sitting down with your "natural" and asking for a "blow out."
- It's being able to play classics on your car radio when other blacks are in the car.
- It's shopping for sun tan oil because you accept that your skin also tans.
- It's telling the white salesperson that her hand inside the stockings do not display the shade that would be produced with black or brown skin.
- It's refusing to accept the table to which a maitre d' hotel takes you because it's next to the kitchen (of special significance for blacks even though whites also might protest).
- It's being able to say you prefer sukiyaki to "chitlins."
- It's also being able to say you want watermelon for dessert.
- It's being one of the first blacks to move into a white neighborhood (because you like the area or it is close to work).
- And it's being able to say you want to move out of the ghetto if you really want to.
- It's telling someone — white or black — without embarrassment that you really care about her/him, or that you really dig something he/she did.
- It's going to a beauty salon that has white beauticians.
- It's asking your newsstand salesperson where you shop to order "Jet" or "Ebony."
- It's asking people (mostly white) not to ruffle your hair as whites frequently do with each other.
- It's not laughing at a joke made about another ethnic group.
- It's taking time at the Christmas party to tell people the correct name for the "nigger toes" they have asked for.
- It's marrying who you want, having white friends if you choose and expressing yourself without putting another person down.

HOW TO USE THIS BOOK

The above examples of assertive behavior from a black perspective are only a few which could be raised. The Survival Ladder exercise in Chapter VI will suggest the infinite variations which can be applied to assertive training. This book attempts to deal with the major issues implicit in each of these examples. How do you prepare a black person — oneself or a client — for assertive living? (Chs. IV and VI). How does a facilitator make certain that the distinctions between passive, aggressive and assertive are applicable to the black experience? (Ch. IV). What white reactions can the assertive black expect and how should these reactions be met? (Chs. IV, VII). What happens in a step-by-step black A-T program? (Ch. VIII). What techniques are best for assisting a black in developing assertive behavior, and which won't work? (Chs. V, VI, VII). What differences are essential to developing an A-T program for blacks rather than whites? (Chs. V, VII, VIII).

As we analyze these types of questions in the pages that follow, the basis of a black A-T (assertive training) program will become clear. The variety of black lifestyles to which such programs need to apply will be evident in the examples and in the discussions which follow. The sensitive facilitator will find the "Survival Ladder" and other sources of examples highly useful to check out the lifestyles and attitudes involved in a particular situation, and to be sure he or she is dealing with black reality.

CHAPTER III

A Foundation for the Black Perspective

> "With few exceptions, black
> professionals have been content to be
> poor carbon copies of their white
> counterparts. This posture has not
> served us well and is a luxury which
> we cannot afford."
> Charles W. Thomas
> *Boys No More*

FRAME OF REFERENCE

A book like this is fraught with many opportunities for misinterpretation. After all, I am advocating treating one segment of our population quite differently from another. This is implicit in my statement that blacks do not benefit from many therapeutic approaches to which whites respond. And I have referred to some of these approaches of counselors and therapists as "white techniques."

I shall not assume that the reader is aware of the major arguments separating black and white therapists, counselors or professional helpers, but will attempt to improve your grasp of the problem by pointing out conflicts and controversies between white and non-white practitioners. The disagreements concern the most effective ways of aiding non-whites to improve their interpersonal skills and social functioning. Conflict may be expressed in a quiet, subtle or professional manner but the conflict is nevertheless present. I see the conflict in college counseling staffs, hospital treatment teams and correctional institutions. It's in social work agencies, probation offices, law enforcement offices, departments of sociology or psychology, and churches.

The problem is epitomized by the position of the blacks quoted in this book but is in no way isolated to blacks. Native Americans, Asians and Spanish-speaking professionals are also upset and indignant. They all express a concern about the lack of sensitivity displayed by white therapists who work with non-white clients but at the same time possess limited knowledge or appreciation for their patients' cultural backgrounds. At a recent California state-wide organizational meeting of ethnic minorities involved in college counseling, the opinion was unanimous. The group representing blacks, Chicanos, native Americans and Asians generally felt that white counselors were doing a poor job of understanding either their non-white clients or non-white co-workers. It was surprising, as a black, to talk with a Japanese- or native-American counselor who experienced the same feelings of distress at the manner in which whites disregarded the importance of cultural variables in relating to, diagnosing, and treating a non-white client. Frequently the relationships of co-workers became strained when the minority professional would point out to their white colleagues the systematic neglect of these cultural and racial factors. The agreed-upon problem was that whites were diligently applying to non-whites culturally biased ideas and theories that they had learned from white teachers, white schools and white communities. Most of these ethnic professionals agreed that their white colleagues exhibited very little sensitivity to, or interest in, the non-white experience.

It is therefore appropriate to ask: "Why are blacks, especially in their in-group conversations, so highly critical of white practitioners?" "What is behind the dialogue of frustration that both groups seem to employ towards each other?" Whites who want to know why blacks always bring up the racial issue and refuse to see "people as people" — and blacks who want to know why whites are so resistant to facing the reality of being "color conscious" products of a racist society. Blacks question how whites avoid racism from creeping into the treatment or counseling situation involving black clients. Whites frequently want to know the same thing as it pertains to black treatment of whites.

To provide the reader with a frame of reference for considering the dispute that exists between white and black practitioners, this chapter presents some critical questions and answers for consideration. The hope is to sensitize the concerned reader as to what all the fuss is about. This is particularly pertinent in this book since I am advocating assertive behavior training from a black perspective.

The reader is entitled to know that this approach to assertive therapy is just the black cultural tip to a white therapeutic iceberg. Examining ideas about behavior (that have been developed primarily from white experiences) and evaluating them as to their value when applied to clients of African heritage is, and has been, an on-going activity for serious black therapists. It should also be an issue of concern for all responsible white clinicians.

On one hand we have ideas about behavior and treatment developed primarily from the experiences of white therapists and white clients. On the other hand we have the attempt to draw on these ideas (called white techniques) that have been found to work with whites and to apply them to black clients *without modification*. The question is, can this be done — and specifically, can this be done with assertive behavior therapy? The answer being given in this book is *no*. And the rationale behind this "no" has a history and background that is seldom if ever discussed in the training programs that produce our counselors, therapists and clinicians. Thus this book is in many ways related to the ongoing effort that black therapists have made to take "white interpretations of behavior" and make sense out of them for their black clients. They have the job of pulling out of white training something of value to the black community — and in the process attempting to improve on both.

Specific suggestions will be made in later chapters with regard to assertive behavior techniques from a black perspective (e.g. approaches to role playing). It is believed that these ideas along with other comments will be better understood if some basic cultural conflicts within the profession are brought out in the open for examination.

Addressing such critical questions and answers will provide a firm background for understanding of suggestions for initiating, conducting, supporting and evaluating an assertive behavior training program for blacks. With the benefit of this exposure to black perceptions, we may avoid misinterpretation or possible rejection of much of what will be discussed later.

A PERSONAL NOTE

A personal comment before we get into the questions and answers. In this section and occasionally in other areas of the book there is the need to "get down." "Get down" is a phrase in the black idiom which indicates one is taking care of business, becoming very serious or dealing with some important issues. While I hope to maintain contact with the average reader, especially the brother or sister from the community, there are some deep issues that may require extra heavy discussion. There are also issues that I feel may need special documentation because of the emotions that are stirred up and the resistance that may be aroused by the topic. The issue of black-white relationships in this society is such a topic. I will therefore tend to treat this area a little differently from others; the reader will notice footnotes, documentation and reference to other sources reflecting my years spent playing the academic game of scholarship. But it's a serious game, for the validity of what you say is, and frequently correctly so, measured and evaluated by your familiarity with the "body of knowledge." Unfortunately for reasons later discussed in this chapter, there is a "white body" and a "black body" with respect to the knowledge. So if I seem to depart into an "academic bag" for awhile it is for two reasons. The first reason is based upon how I am personally divided — part "street nigger" from Harlem and part Ph.D. from white education. The second reason is that there are many readers who are academically-oriented and prone to evaluate the strength of a position primarily by how well grounded it is in other data. The issues to be discussed are important enough, I think, to be presented in the way that can be best heard. The issues I present deserve to be seriously considered and reflected upon by all readers. The ideas are not only mine but are contained in data obtained from other black professionals.

I should also share with the reader that upon first introducing the chapter on black background information I felt somewhat defensive and apologetic. I knew I was going to face questions from my editor and publisher. "Why do you need to go into all of this in order to write about assertive behavior training?" would be the first question. "We thought this was going to be a book about the value of assertive training with blacks!" could be the next comment. And of course I imagined many more questions for which I might not have answers. But all my training, experience and exposure to blacks and whites in relationships that were social, recreational or professional made one thing "perfectly clear" — between the two, whites know very little about blacks. And therefore it just felt wrong to discuss using a specific therapeutic technique (assertive training) with a particular stigmatized group (black people) without some insight into understanding why and how this group may react differently from other populations.

To bolster my apologetic beginning I read and re-read the works of black authors — Saunders Redding, W.E.B. Dubois, Malcolm X, Horace Cayton, to name a few. And I emerged wondering how I could have harbored any doubts. I also had a renewed awareness of how unexposed we are to all sides of the picture in considering the historical roots of the black experience. A shallow, one-sided, white interpretation of the behavioral patterns and perceptions seen in the black clients of today is inadequate. Today's therapist, to become effective, must at least have a basic knowledge of how today's black person is in some ways the result of the past and has had his or her life influenced by the "Jim Crow Halo Effect," skin color, passing, stocking caps, house rent parties and "the dozens," to name just a few realities. *There can be no therapy developed for someone you basically do not understand.*

Thus as I read and wrote, a major part of the problem became more obvious to me: white therapists are frequently attempting to treat clients whom they "think" they know, but in reality they have been miseducated or simply not educated about blacks. We all tend to fill in our lack of knowledge with guesses and assumptions — and we assume a black person has had a somewhat *different* past — but just *how different* the white (and sometimes the black) practitioner doesn't really know. And this failure to understand is because we (both black and white counselors) have ourselves been culturally deprived by exposure to mostly white interpretations of history and the social sciences. It occurs to me that we are in danger of oversimplifying the problem if we don't recognize that the average white therapist is usually functioning with knowledge of blacks that was contained in the sterile, racist-tinged books and uninformed lectures that characterized past (and to a lesser degree current) white education. Thus the "puzzle" is not surprising, but it is clear that exposure is a necessity for anyone seriously contemplating work with a black population.

BLACK ISSUES AND ANSWERS

The following questions and answers have been developed to aid the reader in understanding the black "definition of the situation." We will not be able to understand and treat the black client unless we are more realistically informed about the conditions that have produced certain patterns of behavior among blacks.

Question: *What do black therapists really feel about white therapists?*

Answer: Black practitioners are beginning to publicly express views that in the past were only private observations. The reason black professionals avoided the open expression of views critical of their white colleagues is itself an interesting phenomenon that will be later explained. Typical of the black opinions currently aired are those of Ferdinand Jones. Dr. Jones, a Ph.D. from the University of Vienna and formerly president of the Westchester County Psychological Association in New York, wrote a recent article about the value of the black psychological consultant. He expressed his concern about the pervasiveness and complex depth of white racism as not yet being recognized by establishment psychology or the mental health field in general. Dr. Jones concludes that:

> Consequently, white therapists do not learn to appreciate the racist distortions in themselves and in the rest of the American society. They cannot handle the blackness dimension in their treatment of black patients even with the most human intentions and the most proficient skills. The very sensitive white therapist can become knowledgeable about racism and its effects. He is unusual if he does, but when he does, he begins to see the limitations of his own capacities to deal with the questions surrounding blackness in black patients.[1]

My outspoken colleague and former co-worker Charles W. Thomas is even more pointed in his comments. Dr. Thomas, formerly the national chairman of the Association of Black Psychologists, noted the reaction of white psychologists to the establishment of a black association. He observed that "the white psychologists behaved no differently from other segments of the white population in the characteristic types of reactions toward organized black efforts to change the rules of the social game." Dr. Thomas definitely felt that despite differences in jargon, the activities of white psychologists reflected the social values shared by members of the larger white community. He focused on a traditional gripe of black practitioners when he stated:

The effect of distorting or ignoring the experiences of non-white people maintains the self-serving interests of the dominant social group. Paternalistic exhortation has become characteristic of white social scientists working with non-whites. What these scientists select for attention are the isolated, trivial, or marketable elements of the non-white experience.[2]

These thoughts are being loudly echoed by blacks in all regions of the country. In the East, Thomas Gordon, at my alma mater Temple University says that instead of service to black people, white psychology has been flagrantly self-serving and opportunistic. He even describes the exploitive attitude of white psychologists toward black clients as having "the motive of the vampire rather than those of the advocate."[3] He talks about black people being used indiscriminately as human guinea pigs to further the "scholarly" ambitions and success striving of white social scientists. Hayes and Banks point out that the "inability or unwillingness of whites to examine their behavior or the behavior of their black clients is the fundamental problem from which other problems arise in the counseling of black students."[4] The late Ed Barnes was also concerned about identity problems of black students who work with white counselors.[5] In fact, Grier and Cobbs observe that "White clinicians may unconsciously withdraw from an intimate knowledge of a black man's life because placing themselves in the position of the patient, even mentally, is too painful." They conclude that " . . .such an intimate knowledge of the patient is vital to diagnosis and treatment, in its absence of the patient suffers."[6]

That these feelings of black practitioners are a reflection of reality is occasionally attested to by even white professionals. For example, E. Earl Baughman, in discussing the significance of the white man's perspective, observes that "almost all the judgements about psychopathology among black people have been rendered by white dianosticians, and all too often the white professional has not been adequately trained to understand someone living in a subculture very different from his own." Baughman goes on to restate the heart of the problem separating black and white therapists,

If we are concerned with paranoid behavior, for example, can we apply the same criteria to the black man as we do to the white man when the former is likely to experience more persecution and exploitation than the latter? But to make adjustments for cultural differences the diagnostician must have an intimate knowledge of what is "real" within a subculture and how that reality differs from what is true for the larger society. Unfortunately, most of us who are white lack this intimate knowledge of black culture. Therefore, our conclusions about particular forms of psychopathology among blacks are susceptible to considerable error.[7]

The division between black and white professionals is perhaps most symbolically portrayed in the results of a 1967 survey undertaken by the Committee on Equality of Opportunity in Psychology of the American Psychological Association to study "the Negro Psychologist in America."[8] From a nationwide sample of almost 400 black psychologists the study found that black psychologists were not part of the mainstream of American psychology. The major study pointed out that "a sense of inadequacy and fear had worked hand in glove with actual discrimination to insure the isolation of most black psychologists." The isolation of Black psychologists was further revealed by the finding that although 85% of the sample had obtained either the doctorate or masters degree only an estimated 27% of them were members of the American Psychological Association.

The authors of the study observed that "most black psychologists feel themselves, and until recently were, alienated from American psychology because of the totality of what it means to be black." Many respondents noted the absence of blacks holding APA office and presenting papers at conventions. Immediately it could be said that black psychologists should be more assertive. The conditions under which one throws off generations of "survival oriented," passive behavior, and the forces against such assertion, will be discussed in later chapters. The purpose here is to expose the reader to the many voices that speak to the issue of the black practitioner's attitude toward his white counterpart. The hope is to provide a sense of the strength, urgency and unity in attitude that black therapists share with regard to the need for modifying and rethinking the application to black clients of certain styles, techniques and therapies (e.g. assertive therapy) that have been found to be effective with whites.

The above discussion may have contained strong words to the reader but they are shared in order to provide an awareness of the frequently "unspoken" gap that separates white and black professionals dealing with people.

Question: *If professional blacks have these views why haven't whites heard them more often?*

Answer: This question touches on insecurity on the part of the whites and fear on the part of blacks. Whites, as perceived by blacks, tend to become very "uptight" and insecure in discussing racial issues in general and their personal biases in particular. Knowing they have been exposed to an educational system and period of training that has only superficially dealt with the black experience, if at all, the white expert on behavior may become very anxious about having that particular area of ignorance exposed. The tendency of the white practitioner therefore, is to play down the importance of racial or cultural factors in dealing with behavior. This attitude is combined with feeling somewhat hostile or disturbed towards the person who continually brings up "the issue." This is what Charles Thomas means when he discusses the effect of the socialization process of most graduate schools that produces the type of person that does not challenge traditional theories. Thus, Thomas concludes, it is questionable whether whites can really engage in a reconceptualization process because "to do so would undermine their own conceptions of self."[9]

The black professional is aware of the resistance whites have to having their "racial unawareness" exposed. Instead of asking a white therapist (or a white counselor) how they modify or rethink their particular approach when the client is black, there is the tendency to "be cool and survive." To let the white man think he knows it all has been a standard axiom in the survival of black people in America. And this "survival technique" is based on reality. Let us not forget that the administrators of most staffs, faculties, offices and departments are white. These are white organizational heads who see themselves as liberal and desirous of reducing controversy within their operation (with many feeling that blacks hired in the spirit of "affirmative action" are ungrateful for bringing up such subjects). Black professional goals and advancement are frequently dependent upon white recommendations, together with the good will of whites, most of whom place an emphasis on "ability to get along with co-workers." All of these factors make up the reality of black perceptions.

The black professionals that I know and have been privileged to work with throughout the United States are unanimous in their observations based upon working with white professional "helpers." When the challenge of rethinking or modifying traditional approaches to meet the needs of black clients is brought up, it is at great personal risk. Impressionistically, whites have been known to over-react, become hostile, defensive and — for blacks contemplating career advancement — professionally dangerous. So out of fear, and for reasons of survival, blacks are more prone to discuss these issues at in-group caucuses and conferences. Writing about these issues is even more safe than face to face confrontations. Hopefully, exceptions to these styles will become increasingly evident in both groups. Blacks are becoming more professionally assertive (as they feel more secure based upon tenure, black administrative support or black professional organizations) and a few whites more open (for reasons unknown to this writer). Therefore, just as this book presents a modified approach to assertive training for use with black clients, it is representative of a growing non-white trend toward reconceptualizing and challenging all theories which evolved from a white perspective.

From the classical schools of thought to current behavioral fads, black practitioners are becoming representative of the skeptical non-white professional who is evaluating an approach in terms of its validity to members of the black community. The problem may be old, but I believe the professional Third World

unity and urgency is new. We will see an increasing challenge to
the theories of personality and behavior. The theories of Freud,
Jung, Lewin, Rogers, Skinner, Perls, Maslow, Cooley and Mead
may be in for a rude re-evaluation.

An example of this new questioning is the analysis of Wade
W. Nobles (1973) with regard to applying traditional social
psychological theories to the development of a black self-
concept. Nobles points out that in considering previously
published investigations (including Mead's symbolic
interactional approach) it is highly probable that these
researchers are unable to take into account the "African reality"
of black people living in America. Nobles feels that the notion of
self for peoples of African descent is not captured by Western
scholars. The Western conception of self relates more to the "I"
while the African view requires looking at self more as "we."
Nobles concludes that "The inability of these researchers to
document this aspect of black social reality casts doubt on their
ability to understand and/or document other social psychological
questions in the black community." This phenomenon is also
pointed out by the well-known black psychiatrist Franz Fanon,
who pointed out the disparity between a black person's reality
and the viewpoint of psychoanalytic works to which he (Fanon)
was exposed.[10]

Question: *Who or what is Jim Crow and what does it have to do with
therapy from a black perspective?*
Answer: The special sensitivities and delicate shades of meaning that
confront a therapist working with a black client are frequently
related to a life style heavily influenced by Jim Crow. In fashioning
an assertive training program beneficial to blacks, the 'Jim Crow
Halo Effect' must be understood. It is frequently not talked about
and has somewhat been repressed, overlooked or temporarily
forgotten — by both blacks and whites. But its awesome impact
still has meaning for understanding the individual or group
behavior of black people — and its effect may be lingering in the

theraputic relationship. Explaining and analyzing Jim Crowism is a beginning in opening the reader's eyes to the basic reasons why there is great psychological distance between blacks and whites today. As we look at Jim Crowism we may get an inkling as to how the two worlds began to separately evolve — each one racially, culturally, socially and psychologically isolated from the other. Blacks were isolated from a white world and left to fashion their own reality. For Jim Crow refers to the legal segregation of blacks from whites in everyday life "from the cradle to the grave."

The origin of the term 'Jim Crow' is generally associated with the song and dance routine of Thomas Don Rice, a famous white "blackface" minstrel of the 1830's. Gradually the words "Jim Crow," from one of Rice's songs came to be applied to the legal segregation of blacks from whites.

These Jim Crow laws were enacted in the South between 1890 and 1910. Thus they are particularly important in understanding the black experience because in 1900 nearly 90% of the black population lived in the South. These laws have made an indelible imprint upon the behavior, feelings, and perceptions of blacks with regard to whites; behavior, feelings, and perceptions that have been handed down from generation to generation and contain one key ingredient — survival — how to survive despite the white man.

As C. Vann Woodward has pointed out:
The extremes to which caste penalties and separation were carried in parts of the South (resembled) South Africa. In 1909 Mobile passed a curfew law applying exclusively to blacks and requiring them to be off the streets by 10 p.m. The Oklahoma legislature in 1915 authorized its Corporation Commission to require telephone companies to maintain separate booths for white and colored patrons. North Carolina and Florida required that textbooks used by the public school children of one race be kept separate from those used by the other, and the Florida law specified separation even while the books were in storage. South Carolina for a time segregated a third caste by establishing separate schools for mulatto as well as for white and Negro children. A New Orleans ordinance segregated white and Negro prostitutes in separate districts. Ray Stannard Baker found Jim Crow Bibles for Negro

witnesses in Atlanta courts and Jim Crow elevators for Negro passengers in Atlanta buildings ... The practice often anticipated and sometimes exceeded the laws ... there is more Jim Crowism practiced in the South than there are Jim Crow laws on the books.[11]

Likewise, whites have developed a certain behavior and perception of blacks strengthened by the attitudes of their Southern white brothers — and sisters (not to be chauvinistic). And these characteristics were handed down also from generation to generation with one major theme — white supremacy. The word may at first glance sound out of place until we look at the reactions to busing in Boston or examine our own feelings as parents when white daughters date black sons — regardless of how professional we consider ourselves.

Therefore the practitioner of today is faced with the challenge of being sensitive to blacks in therapy having a reality that may be generally different from those representing a white population. Such differences will frequently contain a value system that was developed for purposes of surviving under the oppression of Jim Crowism. The environment south of Washington, D.C., in which blacks of that day grew up and lived, contained public signs everywhere, painted or handwritten, that were designed to constantly remind them of their skin color and subordination. These were public symbols of a black person's inferior position as designated by law.

With a focus on conditions below the Mason-Dixon Line we should not forget the reality of discrimination in the North as Takaki has noted:

As Leon Litwack has demonstrated in *North of Slavery: The Negro in the Free States, 1790-1860,* the black person was the unfortunate victim of oppressive *de jure* as well as *de facto* discrimination and segregation.

Everywhere in the North, black children usually attended separate and inferior schools. Black people were barred from most hotels and restaurants, and they has separate sections in theatres and churches, invariably in the back. Transportation facilities often were segregated. The street car company in Philadelphia, for example, ruled that Negroes would be allowed to ride only on the front platform. New York City had separate bus cars — one for whites, one for blacks. Negroes who used the New York ferryboats were forced to stay on deck at all hours and in all weather conditions ... an increasing number of black abolitionists adopted a separatist position during the 1850s. Profoundly alienated from white America, militant black leaders like Martin Delany advocated black emigration to South America and Africa. They declared that there was no hope for the black man in America, and that he must find his identity in a black country.[12]

The legal sanction supported racial separation that extended to churches, schools, housing, jobs, eating and drinking. Segregation by law included all forms of public transportation, sports, recreation, hospitals, orphanages, prisons, asylums, funeral homes, morgues and cemeteries. Signs that said "whites only" and "colored" were on entrances, exits, water fountains, restrooms, waiting rooms, ticket windows, pay windows, theatres and water buckets. Some roadside cafes had holes cut at the side for the "colored people" who were not allowed inside. It was always general practice in the South when driving long distances, for blacks to carry their own food and not expect to use the toilets at most gas stations for fear of a conflict with young white gas station attendants who were "asserting" themselves.

Although born and raised in New York City my own experiences with Jim Crow laws have been those of any other black traveling south. I felt it as a child being told to leave a clean railroad coach in Washington, D.C. to be forced into an overcrowded, older, rundown railroad car for "colored only." I watched my aunt in Richmond, Virginia go to the bathroom outdoors because she was refused the use of a public restroom. In Fayetteville, North Carolina I was screamed at by a white salesgirl because my two-year old son drank out of a "white only" water fountain. I had a pistol pointed in my face when I came out of a "white" men's room at a gas station. The attendant said, "The sign says men, that don't mean you, boy, understand." Having this happen to you in front of your wife and two children (before the other three were born) can deeply affect your perceptions of people and society. You can come to fear your own aggression and know there is no such thing as "acceptable assertion." So you develop a mask that few may penetrate — even white therapists who would be embarrassed to see themselves as part of "white oppression."

The standardized reactions of black people to this oppressive type of environment contributed to making up what could be called a black personality that in many ways is different from a white personality. Psychological personality tests today have problems based on a failure to take into account significant differences in the socialization process of black people as being stigmatized and segregated from white people.

These Jim Crow laws along with slavery, lynching, the ridicule of skin color, hair, facial features and the rejection of black culture, formulate the roots of the Black Experience in America. To attempt treating a black client while ignoring these roots is like counseling a deaf mute without understanding sign language. *The person (black or white) who does not study and remember the dehumanizing conditions that have shaped the perceptions of black people in their struggle for survival, is completely handicapped in comprehending, communicating with or relating to a brother or sister (or black client).* I now see how foolish it is to talk to a white audience that has no background for understanding "what black people want."

I am not talking about the need for a Freudian-type psychoanalytic analysis of a black client. Neither am I ignoring the value of dealing with the "now," the present problem of "unfinished business" as the Gestalt therapists would advocate. I am talking about what is "normal" behavior for a black person although it is different from the standard behavior of a white. It is behavior that is correct and appropriate given the generations of exposure to the treatment embodied in Jim Crowism. It is behavior that has been described by terms such as cultural paranoia or the "Black Norm" discussed by Grier and Cobbs in their book *Black Rage.* It is also behavior that is difficult to study and evaluate since it is highly complex. This complexity reflects the multitude of situations and conditions to which a black person must adjust in seeking to become physically safe and pychologically healthy in a society that has stigmatized blacks as inferior. These modes of adjustment vary according to whether or not the black person is an adult or a child, has particular religious affiliation, is male or female, has light or dark skin, is working class or professional, lives in the South or in another locality.

Thus it is recognized that the experiences of a fair skinned, male, Catholic black Ph.D. in Massachusetts may in many ways be different from those of a dark skinned, Baptist, female, domestic in Mississippi. The point here is that what they share as a commonality is frequently more important than the differences. (Malcolm X summed up the essence of such shared commonalities when he posited the question, "What do they call a black man with a Ph.D?" And he answered, "A nigger.")

BLACK STYLES — 10 CHARACTERISTICS

At this point the logical connection between examining the psycho-historical background of blacks and the development of a more meaningful approach to assertive therapy should again be clarified. Put as simply as possible, much of the behavior of a black client (verbal and non-verbal) that the facilitator is confronted with and perplexed by has evolved over a long period of adjustment to various forms of white oppression. Traditional assertive therapy techniques will often not reach or be relevant to a black person who has had a lifestyle conditioned by the "Jim Crow Halo Effect." From my experience and observation, a black person will be different from the white client in possessing one or more of the following characteristics:

1. Bi-dialectical, which means a knowledge of standard English as well as a familiarity with or emphasis upon black language or non-standard English;
2. Cultural paranoia, a general distrust of whites until proven otherwise;
3. A preoccupation with race and its importance;
4. A seething aggression and pent up anger and rage;
5. A lack of loyalty to white institutions or organizations;
6. Conflict in whether to talk "white" or "black";
7. An alertness to preferential treatment given to whites;
8. An ability to "fake it" with white people and not reveal self;

9. A sensitivity to non-verbal cues such as body posturing, manner of walk, use of eyes, sucking of teeth and facial expressions;

10. A suspiciousness and unconvinced attitude concerning patriotism, authority, the value of law and hard work.

It should be noted, less these characteristics be misused, that there is nothing about these general patterns that is instinctive, biological or hereditary. As I have been exposed to these behaviors, I have seen these characteristics altered or eliminated by virtue of changes in social environmental conditions. Thus these characteristics are not inherent but are subject to change in relation to such variables as social class, ethnic identity or region (such as moving to a different locality or country).

The position taken here however, is that in order for a therapist to be therapeutically innovative and psychologically comfortable with a black client, rather than just patronizing, there must be a deep awareness of why and how that black person behaves differently. An important part of the answer involves the years of segregation and discrimination that have produced certain priorities and survival techniques that are important to blacks but can be threatening to whites. To just use one example, we can take the third black characteristic mentioned — a preoccupation with race and its importance. As Stikes found in assessing the needs of black students, "the issue of race was a consuming experience . . . they were suspicious of white teachers, students, and other personnel . . ."[13] This finding is generally true of the black population. As we have already seen, the Jim Crow environment makes it impossible to forget about race — in fact blacks must remember and never forget the importance of skin color if they are to survive. But while race and its implications are of overwhelming importance to blacks, whites prefer not to discuss it. An outspoken white mother and author succinctly states:

> To our generation, racism is what sex was to our parents — 'nice people' did not discuss it. I had never heard a bigoted phrase from my neighbors, and I feel sure they would have been as embarassed if their children said 'nigger' as my mother would have been if I had said 'masturbate' or 'intercourse'. For both generations, sex and racism existed — but suppressed and secret.[14]

Unfortunately what Mrs. Stalvey has observed about her white neighbors is prevalent among white professional helpers. I, along with many of my black colleagues have seen and felt the resistance of white professionals when racial or cross-cultural topics are introduced.

WHITE SKILLS AND BLACK CLIENTS

So here we have the problem. The majority of clinicians and "professional helpers" of today are puzzled: they know very little about the historical aspects of the Black Experience which would help them to provide a better service to black clients. The history and social science of "white studies" as taught by white teachers certainly did not provide a balanced interpretation. And the graduate schools and universities where training takes place are usually barren of any ethnic or multi-cultural input. This is not to even mention the need for an analysis of the historical context of racism in America as related to the personality and mental health of blacks and whites. So we therefore have large numbers of practitioners who "know all they want to know" about blacks and the psycho-historical past. And the problem is getting worse. There are young prospective counselors that I teach in graduate school who know little and care less as to what the term Jim Crow means or represents. They are shocked to hear that not long ago blacks were not allowed to play football, baseball or basketball with whites and that the United States had separate armies and Red Cross blood banks for blacks and whites. Yet these same puzzled students want to "understand" black behavior (some even persist in referring to "the Negro Problem").

To some extent it should be obvious that an assertive behavior program for a population that has a background of Jim Crowism must be, in basic ways, different from an approach geared to meet the needs of the average white client. Because of the Jim Crow Halo effect a black client more frequently comes to the assertive therapy facilitator with characteristics that are different in order of priority, intensity and relevance to survival. The speech and word usage of the facilitator take on particular importance. Unless sensitive to the points already discussed, therapists may not know how they are "turning off" black clients. They may be unaware of how American society has put special meaning on certain words and social situations. Words or phrases like *boy, auntie, Uncle Tom, you people, sold down the river, Chinaman's chance, jew him down, scot free* and *not seeing someone in a coon's age,* when spoken by whites provide blacks with special clues about the speaker. Comments about blushing to a group trying out assertive training exercises has particular meaning to a black client. From having one's head rubbed in a good-natured manner (which blacks do not like) by a white therapist, to being paired with a white partner in an assertiveness training group, the Jim Crow Halo Effect will frequently be present.

FOOTNOTES

[1] Jones, Ferdinand, "The black psychologist as consultant and therapist," in *Black Psychology.* Reginald L. Jones, (Ed.), N.Y.: Harper & Row, ©1972, p. 371. Used by permission.

[2] Thomas, Charles W., "The system — maintenance role of the white psychologist," *Journal of Social Issues,* ©1973, 29, 59. Used by permission.

[3] Gordon, Thomas, "White and black psychology," *Journal of Social Issues,* 1973, 29, 88-89.

[4] Hayes, William A., and Banks, William M., "The nigger box of a redefinition of the counselor's role." In Reginal Jones, (Ed.), *Black Psychology,* N.Y.: Harper & Row ©1972, pp. 225-226. Used by permission.

[5] Barnes, Edward J., "Counseling and the black student: the need for a new view." In *Black Psychology,* Reginald Jones, (Ed.), N.Y.: Harper & Row, ©1972, p. 219.

[6] Grier, William H., and Cobbs, Price M., *Black Rage.* N.Y.: Basic Books, ©1968, p. 156. Used by permission.

[7] Baughman, E. Earl, *Black Americans,* N.Y.: Academic Press, ©1971, p. 69. Used by permission. (These comments, I am sure, are particularly welcomed by the over 200 black patients at Atascadero State Hospital in California. This group, with whom I have worked, are exposed to diagnosis and treatment in an institution that has at this date no full-time professional black staff person to interpret the meaning of the black experience to those who are the white decision-makers — deciding when a black patient is "adjusted" enough to return to his community.)

[8] Wispe, Lauren, et. al. "The negro psychologist in America," in *The Psychological Consequences of Being a Black American,"* Wilcox, Roger Clark, Ed., N.Y.: John Wiley and Sons, 1971, pp. 449-465.

[9] Thomas, Charles W., "The system — maintenance role of the white psychologist." *Journal of Social Issues,* 1973, 29, 60.

[10] Fanon, Frantz B., *Black Skin, White Masks,* N.Y.: Grove Press, 1967.

[11] *The Strange Career of Jim Crow* (Third Revised Edition) ©1955, 1957, 1974 by C. Vann Woodward. N.Y.: Oxford University Press. Used by permission.

[12] Takaki, R., "The black child savage in ante-bellum America." In Nash, G.B. & Weiss, R. (Eds.) *The Great Fear: Race in the Mind of America.* N.Y.: Holt, Rinehart and Winston, Inc., ©1970, pp. 101-102. Used by permission.

[13] Stikes, Scully C., "A conceptual map of black student development problems." *Journal of Non-White Concerns,* Oct. 1975, p. 26. See also B. McGwine, "Black visions, white realities," *Change,* 1972, 3 (3), 28-33, and A. McCord and C. Willie, *Black Students at White Colleges.* N.Y.: Praeger, 1972.

[14] Stalvey, L.M., *Getting Ready . . . The Education of a White Family in Inner City Schools.* N.Y.: William Morrow and Company, Inc., ©1974, p. 17. Used by permission.

CHAPTER IV

Assertive Behavior and Black Lifestyles

> For his own survival, then, (a black
> man in America) . . . must develop a
> cultural paranoia in which every
> white man is a potential enemy unless
> proved otherwise and every social
> system is set against him unless he
> personally finds out differently.
> William H. Grier
> Price M. Cobbs
> *Black Rage*

THE BLACK EXPERIENCE

Imagine a scene in which a black young man in his early twenties is cruising along on a late summer evening. He is kicking back, digging the sounds of Beethoven on his tape deck. Deciding to see what his partners are doing, he goes by a friend's house. Three of his friends are home, ask if they can cruise with him and jump into the car. As they drive off, one of the group loudly asks the driver, "What's that shit you playin' man, why don't you turn on some sounds?"

His friend in the back seat picks up the theme and adds, "Yeah, baby, we don't need no fucked up white music bendin' our minds up." Everybody laughs and there is good natured palm slappin' among those who just "ran it down" to the driver.

How could that young man, who wanted to listen to Beethoven on his tape deck, have been helped by assertive training? What kind of assertive training did he need that could enable him to be assertive in contrast to aggressive or non-assertive? Conversely, what type of assertive training would be useless or even harmful to him in dealing with his environment? These questions are asked because traditional white-oriented therapies have had a lot of good-sounding suggestions that don't work for blacks. Following in their path, assertive training also has some great ideas, such as: "Express feelings honestly and openly," "Act in your own best interest and stand up for yourself without undue anxiety," and "Exercise your own rights without putting people down." But for blacks the issue has always been, how do you translate those high sounding objectives into the everyday activities of blacks folks? As some of my patients at Atascadero State

Hospital's Black Project would ask, "Hey, Dr. Cheek, how can you break that shit down to something I can use — you know, like get my thang across to people without them gettin' bent out of shape?" Thus, the challenge is, how does one make those ideas and objectives of assertive training attainable (not just desirable or meaningful) to those who must live the Black Experience? Many of the lofty ideals and suggested behaviors offered by traditional practitioners are greeted with raised eyebrows and questioning glances. Many blacks with non-white clients wonder how all "that shit" would work with the folk that *they* have to deal with.

NEW REQUIREMENTS FOR OLD PROBLEMS

If assertive training is to realize its full potential of being of value to people regardless of ethnic or cultural background, then it must deal with problems that have up to now been ignored. From a black perspective this means that at least three conditions must be met:

1) A willingness to modify the traditional white middle class focus and assumptions;
2) A willingness to accept the reality and legitimacy of the Black Experience (Jim Crow Halo Effect) in reformulating the approach for black clients;
3) An openness to exploring ways of self-expression that may differ from conventional communication.

In fact, these three requirements are really a true test for *any* therapeutic approach that is to be translated to meet the needs of black people.

In mentioning the traditional white middle class focus of assertive behavior training (along with all the other therapies and techniques of the helping professions I am asking a fundamental question. Do those who provide a psychological or mental health service *really* want to include everyone? Do we really want to help the black, the poor, the lower class, the working class, the poorly educated, the delinquent and imprisoned? Which of our psychological theories, therapies and techniques are really meant for them? Or are we assuming that all our methods or theories can really benefit only the white middle-class-oriented patient who has been the traditional client?

My assumption is that there are many professionals and laymen who would like to know ways of aiding *all* people regardless of race or social position. This is where I feel assertive training can meet the need. Since a critique of psychological theories is not the purpose of this book, I will just say that some theories have more built-in cultural biases than others. In like manner, some approaches are tested or standardized upon white populations or discussed in terms of reported results in treating only white clients. My contention is that assertive training provides an approach which is relatively free of cultural biases and therefore can be of maximum benefit to the black community.

Despite A-T's potential, the way it is practiced by many whites can stamp it as useless to many blacks. As my man in the Black Project would say, "How can you break that shit down to somethin' I can use?" Thus, although there may be a willingness to modify the traditional white middle class focus there is an obstacle in the fact that most practitioners of today don't know how to "break it down" for use by a black population.[15] This is where sensitivity to the feelings of the average black person seeking treatment is necessary — sensitivity and understanding of the black client who will reflect varying degrees of suspicion, resistance, doubt, hostility and lack of confidence in the therapeutic process. To truly break assertive training down for relevance and use by black clients, these feelings and attitudes must be considered.

CHANGING TO ASSERTIVENESS — THE FIRST FIVE STEPS

With these thoughts in mind, the basic approach of assertive training from a black perspective can be considered in terms of 10 steps — the first five steps are for purposes of preparation and the last five steps are for purposes of action. The action steps will be discussed in Chapter VIII. It is first necessary to look at the five preparation steps — the beginning phase that orients the black client for later assertive action. These initial steps can modify the conventional assertive training approach so that it begins to address the needs of the black client. The five basic preparation steps are:

1) Introduce and explain assertive training as something that can benefit most people; assess anxiety level of client (Use Assertive Inventory, Chapter VI).

2) Obtain racial description of the "somebody" or "target person" with whom the client wants to be assertive. (Use Survival Ladder, Chapter VI).
3) Determine tendency to use black, white or both language styles (Use Black-White Language Questionnaire, Chapter VI).
4) Discuss the meaning of being assertive, aggressive or passive as related to the Black Experience. Interpret the 10 black characteristics, the Jim Crow Halo effect and the Psycho-Historical roots of black-white relationships (see "Before You Work With Blacks" questionnaire, Chapter VI).
5) Discuss the social reality of black-black and black-white assertiveness (use Group Awareness Profile, Chapter VI).

As the reader can see, each step, except for the introductory statement, deals directly with the interracial realities that consistently confront the black client. This is an area that has been given no attention by the popular proponents of assertive training, although it is crucial to success in helping black clients. Also, each step is accompanied by a suggested inventory or questionnaire as a guideline for increased effectiveness and sensitivity. Most important, of course, is the question of whether or not the practioner, black or white, is basically prepared to deal with black clients. This issue is addressed in the "Before You Work With Blacks" questionnaire, which suggests the minimum level of familiarity with black subject matter which is necessary to be of real service to a black client. However, if the assertive training facilitator has the willingness to depart from the conventional mode of being assertive and a real acceptance of the importance and value of the Black Experience, then the utilization of the suggested steps can make this approach emotionally and psychologically beneficial to a large segment of the black population.

Of crucial importance in modifying assertive training techniques to fit the needs of black clients is our willingness and ability to revise and broaden our ideas about what is the "right thing to say" in an assertive message. The *right* thing may only prove to be the *white* thing. And this would immediately take away the value of assertive training for blacks (remember the Jim Crow Halo Effect).[16] Now I realize that for many facilitators the assertive training process includes having clients concentrate on particular situations and develop their own "natural style" of being assertive. But if assertive training techniques are to become truly beneficial to the wide range of cultural attitudes and social differences that are represented in black people, some basic assumptions must be re-evaluated. Most therapists have worked so long with one type of middle-class-oriented client, that they accidentally fall into some habits of thought, convenient jargon and old assumptions. It is easy to forget that there are many who think, function and respond differently to the identical words and methods that previously brought success with a white subject. Thus, in teaching assertiveness to many blacks and non-middle class oriented groups, the therapist must be prepared to leave behind a format that uses procedures, expressions and cliches that were meaningful in past situations. Asking a client to concentrate on a particular situation and develop a "natural assertiveness" assumes, among other things, that the person will allow the therapist into his/her world of reality. When that same person is asked to watch someone as an effective model, it is assumed that the components of the model's style, and to a lesser degree the model's words, can be of value. To tell the person not to be loudly aggressive or offensive, again assumes commonly accepted interpretation of what is "loud" and what is "offensive." I am refering to such cautions as those offered by my colleagues Alberti and Emmons who suggest that the client be asked to consider alternative responses that are "less offensive."

Thus, to place a young black person, like the driver of that car, into an assertive training group, without attention to these issues may be to fail to prepare him properly to deal effectively and assertively with his peers. Likewise, a *book* which would provide that young black person with attainable and useful guidance must take into account the Black Experience.

WHY A WHITE APPROACH CAN FAIL

The reasons for failure in white-oriented assertive training when used with black clients can easily be traced to one or all of the following:

1) The facilitator's lack of preparation for dealing with the black client's high resistance to self disclosure.[17]
2) The facilitator's unawareness of the relationship between the client's exploration of self and the effects of the therapist's race.[18]
3) Ignoring the many problems involved in having a white facilitator function as a model for a black client.[19]
4) Ignoring the possibility that aggressive actions in terms of being "loud" or "offensive" may be defined or labeled differently by conventional whites and non-conventional blacks.
5) A general unawareness of the real world of the black client in which race, social barriers, survival and bi-dialectic speech (talking black or talking white) have high priority and concern.

One of the promises of assertive training especially for blacks, is in helping young (and old) people resist their peers and the pressure of "going along with the crowd." It seeks to help provide and strengthen their right to choose, allowing them to resist drugs, alcohol, smoking, stealing cars, and fear of being called "square" or different. In addition, it can be used by black adults who fail to express their real selves for fear of being labeled "Tom," "Bourgeois" or "oreo." Of course lack of assertion also functions for those blacks who fear the labels "militant," "activist" or "radical."

We therefore again face the critical question: "What form of assertive training did the young black driver need to experience that could enable him to be assertive?" The answer is both complex and simple. The simple part is, that the young man needed exposure to a facilitator who had the ability to implement the five basic preparation steps which would automatically include a respect for the use of black language. Because of the particular situation, an effective assertive message would have to be couched in terms of a black message that could be properly understood (decoded) by his black peers. "Talking white" at that particular time would have been disastrous.

What is white talk and what is black language and what are the rules that guide appropriate usage? This part is complex; the Jim Crow Halo effect has kept blacks and whites separated to the point of each using the same language, English, but using it differently. Black language patterns make use of words in everyday situations that mainstream whites consider offensive — although the "less offensive" terms like "cool," "funky," "hip" and "right on" have been conveniently borrowed. But if a facilitator is to really get into the black world that is produced by closed eyes in a period of concentration, then the earthy "at home" words of the the black experience may appear: "Nigguh," "mothafucka," "lighten up," "heavy shit," and "Honkey" plus a variety of filler words such as "you know," "like" and "I mean" which are part of *signifying, cappin* and *rappin* in the black tradition. It is this reality that blacks hesitate to reveal to white facilitators, assuming, in view of past experiences, that "they ain't ready to deal with it." The black person "knows" that the dominant white group has already judged black people, their values, speech and lifestyle as inferior. The black client's attitude frequently questions why he or she should re-experience the shock, dismay and patronizing comments of a white facilitator. More on language styles in Chapter V.

I hope that through the use of the basic steps presented, assertive training can be so structured that a black client will be exposed to someone who is both black-oriented and already familiar with the black reality and black language styles. This type of facilitator can more easily elicit the participation of black clients (since they are not revealing something foreign, unknown and potentially shocking) in developing assertive alternatives. This type of facilitator will be less judgmental about the words of an assertive message and be more capable of modeling assertive responses, *appropriate* for the target person (the individual to whom the message is directed). If our young driver participated in such an assertive training session we could easily imagine him saying. "Hey, man, why you want to jump in my car and start all that old bullshit? Why don't you just lighten up, let me finish diggin' on this — cause you know it is my car and you can always get you ass out and walk — you dig?" I am sure the passengers would get the message and no doubt be cool — at least for awhile.

FOOTNOTES

[15] Many black counselors have warned that real communication between the white counselor and black client depends upon the counselor becoming sufficiently acquainted with the client's cultural background to permit an in depth understanding of black verbal and nonverbal patterns of communication (body posturing, hand gestures, and facial expressions). The work of practitioners like Edward Barnes has cautioned us that a counselor who has primarily a middle class orientation may over-emphasize verbal ability and self-disclosure, and thereby fail to understand the client's non-verbal communication. This could result in the counselor perceiving the person as "nonverbal" or "unable to relate." See Edward J. Barnes, "Counseling and the black student: The need for a new view" in *Black Psychology*, Reginald L. Jones, Ed., N.Y.: Harper & Row, 1972, p. 218.

[16] "We suggest that this inability or unwillingness of whites to examine their own behavior and the effects of their behavior on the behavior of their black clients is the fundamental problem from which other problems arise in the counseling of black students." William A. Hayes and William M. Banks, "The nigger box or a redefinition of the counselor's role" in *Black Psychology*, Reginald Jones, Ed., pp. 225 and 226.

[17] The hesitancy of blacks to fully disclose themselves has been consistently demonstrated in research. See Jourard and Laskow, "Some factors in self-disclosure," *Journal of Abnormal Psychology*, 1958, 56, 91-98. See also George H. Wolkan, Sharon Moriwaki and Karen J. Williams, "Race and social class as factors in the orientation toward psychotherapy" in *Journal of Counseling Psychology*, 1973, Vol. 20, No. 4, pp. 312-316. They found that since blacks are unwilling to reveal themselves even to each other, the lack of disclosure on the personal level could indicate more need for professional help.

[18] Carkhuff, R.R. and Pierce, R., "Differing effects of therapist race and social class upon patient depth of self exploration in the initial interview." *Journal of Counseling Psychology*, 1967, 31, pp. 632-634.

[19] It should be somewhat obvious that a black client using a white counselor as a role model will encounter many dangers. Such a relationship could contribute to an identity crisis as well as conflict in the expression of racial attitudes. The black counselor is less likely to present such a conflict for the black client since usually they have lived a similar experience. This problem has been commented upon frequently by black observers like the late Edward J. Barnes. See Edward J. Barnes, "Counseling and the black student" op. cit. p. 219.

CHAPTER V

Black Rappin and Cappin

"We...(Black people)...exist in two
cultural worlds and in two different
societies at the same time, without
being totally a part of either."
Julius Lester
Look Out Whitey, Black Power's Gon'
Get Your Mama!

BLACK MESSAGE — MODE AND STYLE

Frequent reference has been made to black language. For our purposes, black language is defined as the body of words used and understood by large numbers of American black people as a special way of relating to each other. Black language is frequently used in ways that cannot be easily understood by whites and in this sense is consistent with its slavery roots. Other definitions of Black Language include "...the language of speaking in the black community...(The English language which it is partly derived from is considered a second language)...The Mother Tongue of the Black Community." (Andrews and Owens, 1973) Brother Andrews also notes that "Slaves who dared to speak of rebellion or even freedom usually were severely punished. Consequently, Negro slaves were compelled to create a semi-clandestine vernacular in the way that the criminal underworld had historically created words to confound law enforcement agents." Another author mentions that "In many respects, the development of verbal behavior in black Americans parallels the development of their music (another form of oral expression). Throughout the years blacks have evolved forms of expression which are unique, spontaneous, and extremely communicative." (Haskins and Butts, 1973).

Social scientists have recognized that different modes of speech produce different modes of thought. This is the basis of the inability of many blacks and whites who have different modes of speech to communicate effectively with each other. These two groups use different styles of speech in which the same or similar terms may represent entirely different meanings depending upon whether one is black or white.

An example of such a semantic change is in the word, 'bad', where the conventional meaning is reversed so that 'bad' means *good* or *the best* in black language. It is very common among blacks to hear how "that dude had on some bad vines" (good looking clothes) or "that group played some bad sounds" (good music). But of course there are times when the black person may use bad in its more conventional meaning e.g. "that chick had some bad breath" or "I woke up with a bad head." As Brothers Andrews and Owens point out so well,

> . . .the words alone are not what makes the communication of the language. The gestures, inflections and nuances of the people are necessary for what is being said to be complete. Tne language is only fully actualized when the words become sounds and the body gives them their impetus and direction.[20]

There is a long list of words that have one meaning in white speech and quite another meaning as used by blacks. Black language is more than just slang, it is a creative and physical language where words like *bodacious, bulldagger, hinkty, poon tang, sashay,* and *cracker* have meanings of long standing and a certain sound when spoken. Haskins and Butts have noted,

> Some of the other 'Americanisms' that appear to have an African or probably African origin are jazz, jitter, and jitter-bug, hep (or hip), banjo, boogie-woogie, jam (as in jam session), jive, to goose, to bug someone, to lam (go), to dig (to understand or appreciate), uh-huh, and uh-huh (for yes and no), ofay and honkie (names for the white man), cocktail, guy and bogus. Many such words are direct-loan words from Africa; others are metamorphosed African words; and still others are direct translations.[21]

Other characteristics of black language are the double preposition *(I'm gonna make it on to the crib)*; the adverbial prepositional phrase *(Get on out the way)*; double pronoun reflexive *(I'm gonna get me a drink)* along with other patterns that make up separate speech forms. Andrews and Owens (1973) provide a full and detailed discussion of these and other black language forms.

Black language gets the feeling out. It has force, emotion and appeal. It is speech patterns and phonetic sounds together with a certain rhythm and meter that makes it easy to distinguish but difficult to casually imitate. The sound and rhythm is easily heard in the traditional sermons of the black Baptist preacher — in this sense the speeches of the Reverend Martin Luther King were examples of black oratory in its true tradition.

Other traditional aspects of black language include *the dozens* (competitive word game in which the mother or family members are degraded), *signifying* (teasing or provoking people into anger) and *cappin* (in which you top someone's comment or cut someone down with words). There is also the liberal use of words that blacks use with each other in special ways — *blood, nigger, splib* – as well as words reserved for a particular emphasis in special situations, such as *motherfucker*. This word in particular gives whites great trouble; it can be used like no other word in no other way. Andrews and Owens treat its use as a noun, verb, and intensifier. Their account of its varied meanings is amplified in my friend Brother Everett Hoagland's poem (see Appendix I).

Black language lends itself to being spoken with vigor and energy in a tone of voice that has more volume than conventional speech. Perhaps this is why many blacks are considered "loud" by white middle class standards. This could also account for a facilitator judging (perhaps erroneously) the statement of a black client as loud, offensive and aggressive even though the same statement would be appropriate in a black oriented environment. It also relates to black rejection of white language. Andrews and Owens again:

> Black language is one of "Primary Explosion" because guttural forces come strongly into the first syllable of a word. For instance in the word *police*. PO is said with much emphasis, with a long and loud stress of the O. Because of this, last sounds of a word are usually less emphasized or not spoken. This is particularly true with a final D, T, or R. For instance, *their* in English is comparable to *they* in black language: "They come to get they clothes?"[22]

Black playwright Charles Gordonne has said, "I found out early that the English language was designed to defeat people like me. So I tried to abort it" (1970). Also Andrews and Owens observe that many black people have to subconsciously change their thinking in words to communicate with white people. This cultural difference raises two issues that will be examined at greater length later: the value judgment of white facilitators and the meaning of being black-oriented. But for now, we are focusing on black language since the degree to which it is accepted and understood can easily determine the effectiveness or ineffectiveness of an assertive behavior training program.

In contrast to black language, white speech is characterized by a stress on standard grammar and "correct" enunciation. To most blacks, white speech is inclined to be formal in style and nasal, precise or clipped in sound. White conversation is seen by blacks as being usually subdued, "intellectual" sounding and very square, symbolized by expressions like *golly, gee whiz, gosh, heck, holy cow, neat* and *keen.* In a white style of communicating, emotions are controlled and tones are modulated (in other words, quiet). This is not to say that whites cannot be boisterous. But vigorous emotional conversation among whites usually departs from the norm of restraint and inhibition. Blacks suspect that whites only really "get it on" and emotionally express themselves when they have been drinking or when they escape from the presence of people who know them in their routine roles, to places where they are somewhat anonymous (like visits to Harlem or to Mexico). Again contrast in the verbal habits of the two groups is also seen in differences between the content of what is considered a routine topic of conversation, as indicated in the "Black-White Language Comparison" chart.

BLACK-WHITE LANGUAGE COMPARISON
Content (What you talk about)

Black-Black
— white people and their racist attitudes
— coming social events, parties, concerts, music
— past social events
— mutual friends, sexual and romantic activities, gossip
— clothing, planned trips, purchases
— making money, hustling, job opportunities
— being black in America

Black-White
— weather
— school or work
— mutual acquaintances
— sports
— the news, politics, current events
— activities of interest to whites (flower gardening, beer parties, fishing)
— rarely about social events, unless work-related

Style (How you talk about it)

Black-Black	Black-White
— use of slang	— somewhat restrained
— usually lots of laughter	— little or occasional slang
— in-group gestures, palm slapping louder than usual	— awareness of grammar
— Black English (violation of grammar)	
— assumed intimacy	

Function (Why you talk about it)

Black-Black	Black-White
— relaxation	— to get or maintain a position
— mutual interest	— to be seen as capable of getting along
— become better acquainted or maintain friendship	— to be seen favorably for reasons of future promotions or improvement in position (good grade)
	— to not be seen as different
	— mutual interest
	— obtain or keep business connection

These contrasting styles and differing points of emphasis have produced conflict and lack of communication. This has been particularly true of the conditions faced by blacks in therapeutic situations. Black clients are met by white practitioners who apply the only standards they know (typically those taught in professional training which has ignored the black experience). These standards are usually based upon white values and white expectations for judging the appropriateness of verbal and non-verbal behavior. Research has pointed out that black interviewers elicit greater linguistic elaboration than do white interviewers, and that there is low linguistic compatability between black students and white counselors. Such findings lead to the not-surprising conclusion that there is perhaps greater facility in communication among persons who are similar in characteristics.

One researcher concluded that in the interview situation and probably in the larger society, whites are a source of anxiety, they prescribe role behaviors for blacks to enact, and create distances between black and white. (Ledvinka, 1969).

Another research team summarized its results: "These findings indicate strong support for a position that the development of a good counseling relationship between a white counselor and a black student may be difficult. The importance of having black counselors and of having an educational component for white counselors that deals with areas of curriculum related to blacks as well as on the job training is further emphasized." (Bankiotes, et. al., 1972).

Other data are found to generally support the contention that blacks do not feel psychologically comfortable or verbally free in a completely white-oriented clinical or therapeutic situation. For these, and other reasons to be discussed, assertiveness training from a black perspective requires that the values, perceptions and speech patterns of the black community be given recognition and major consideration in developing assertive messages. As could be expected there is a great value in the facilitator being black or having been exposed to training from those who can balance a white orientation with a black perspective. It was with this problem in mind that the "Before You Work With Blacks" Test (Chapter VI) was developed. Hopefully it will help individuals to begin to see the adequacy of their own skills as potential facilitators for black clients.

WHO IS THE TARGET?

While black clients should have their unique American experience and language recognized, it is clear they must be prepared to function in situations outside of the black community. If assertive behavior training is really to be of benefit to blacks in aiding them in their interpersonal affairs, then relationships both in and out of their immediate surroundings must be considered. This means that blacks must deal effectively with the dominant white society. This brings us again to the hard reality of black survival — and the oversight of most popular assertive training advisors. Almost every step-by-step guide to assertive training asks questions about how you would react to someone who cut in front of you in a line, or asked you for a favor, or short-changed you at the supermarket. Situations are analyzed which examine your behavior toward sales clerks and bus drivers or supervisors and bosses. The one factor that is always left out by these authors and advice-givers is the race of the person to whom you are responding: the race of that "someone" who gets in front of you in line or short changes you at the supermarket, the race of that bus driver or of your supervisor. I have previously referred to the absence of interracial discussion by these authors as the flesh-colored band-aid approach. Their basic assumption seems to be that the asserter (communicator) and assertee (target person) are white or that racial differences make no difference!

Failure to note the different interactions that may exist when the assertive behavior is directed to a person of another skin color is either an oversight or denial of the racial consciousness that is traditional in our society. If the race (and skin color) of that someone (be it bus driver, sales clerk, supervisor or boss) is not important to a white person, it certainly is of importance to blacks. Of course, the situation and personality of the person can vary the importance of race (it is well known that there are blacks who act and talk white) but generally speaking there is a foundation and traditional basis for blacks to respond differently to whites than to each other. This appears to be so, if for no other reason than that blacks do not attribute as much power to fellow blacks as they do to whites (which I see as the wrong reason). This assumption unfortunately is part of the Jim Crow Halo Effect and relates to the many years that blacks have adopted the so-called master's view towards themselves as heard in the black expression, "Niggers ain't shit." Although the recent focus on black pride and unity has reduced this problem, it would be dishonest and foolish to say the issue does not continue to exist. Therefore each "someone" mentioned in the routine assertiveness training discussion may conjure up different memories and reactions by a black client depending upon whether the person they concentrate upon is black or white. In the "memory bank" of the black community...

- white bus drivers had the power to shoot, to decide if you rode or how far toward the middle you sat
- white salesclerks first waited on all the white people and usually were discourteous to blacks
- white real estate salesmen offered you the worst housing and usually for the highest price
- white hotel clerks refused to recognize room reservations
- white waiters seated you where you would be out of sight (if they seated you at all)
- white employers paid you less and promoted you last if at all
- not to mention the white policeman whose image in the black mind is well known and persistent.

Again, this is not to say blacks themselves have always treated *each other* fairly. But because of past racial discord and currently unresolved problems, black-white communications are frequently much different in form and content.

Let us take the example of a young black couple looking for a house to buy in a nice area of town. When a white salesperson looks through his listings and says he has nothing available, the husband could respond by

    a. saying "O.K." and leaving (passive)

    b. saying "Listen man — I figured there was probably going to be some racist bullshit when I came in here. I'm not going to waste no time hasslin with you dudes — I'm just going to report your ass — to the government, to the state, to the county and anybody else I can find — and what's left of your white ass I'm going to sue." (aggressive)

    c. asking, "Is it because my wife and I are black that suddenly everything is taken? If so, man, we're going to the State Realtors Board to check you out." (assertive but seen as aggressive by many whites because of the threat)

    d. saying, "You know, I figured by your attitude when we first came in that you weren't going to find any room in that white neighborhood for our black faces." (assertive but may be "heard" as aggressive by whites because of reference to race).

If the sales person happens to be black the husband would probably say,

    a. "Hey brother, later, we know you got to hold on to your gig" (passive)

    b. "Man, you sure a jive motherfucka. You got this little flunky job with these white boys and forgot all about your people. Well ain't this some shit! Well let me tell you baby — you can forget it — you don't have to worry about me — and I'm gon to tell everybody I know not to worry about *you*. (aggressive)

    c. "O.K. brother, you going to take care of me later — I mean you going to let me know when something is available." (assertive)

    d. "Hey brother, what's wrong, they ain't going to let you sell us no place in their lily white neighborhood? Man you best get on the job and get me something?" (assertive — but seeming somewhat aggressive to many whites because of the demand).

In the black-white communication there is the anticipation of prejudice on the part of the white person that accounts for the need to be assertive. In the black-black interaction there is the anticipation that social forces (not the person) dictate the need for assertion. Thus in the black-white confrontation the age old racial problem of the black person being "victimized" or oppressed by whites comes to the surface. This places the dialogue in an "oppressor vs. oppressed" category, while in the black-black situation there is more of a "I am dealing with a dude just like me" attitude. There seems to be more intuitive understanding (and acceptance) that the sales person is controlled by social forces — "they" may take his job away. At the same time there is the type of black-black assertive response that expresses hope and an ethnic expectation. (Black teachers talk about this "brotherly" ethnic expectation in terms of the black "A"). At any rate, the black-black dialogue comes close to the "equal speaks to equal" category while the black-white conversation has a different quality. These differences are characterized in the following chart:

COMPARISON OF
BLACK-WHITE AND BLACK-BLACK INTERACTION

Black-White Interaction	Black-Black Interaction
1. Black sees white person to blame	1. Black sees black person as socially controlled
2. Black will move into "oppressor vs. oppressed" relationship	2. Black will move into equal vs. equal relationship
3. Black will refer to racial *differences* and use terms of potential threat to whites	3. Black will refer to racial *similarity* and use terms like "brother" and "sister" that soften assertiveness
4. Blacks will occasionally "revert" to black language and *intimidate*	4. Black will occasionally "revert" to black language and introduce *humor*
5. Blacks will be sensitive to looking for any *inequality* that may exist between self and whites	5. Black will be sensitive to *looking* for *common ground* that exists between self and black person
6. Blacks will *resent* the use of in-group terms like *nigger, blood* and *member*	6. Black will *accept* the use of in-group terms like *nigger, blood,* and *member*
7. Blacks will attribute *greater harm* and survival threat to an interaction that ends negatively	7. Black will attribute *little harm* or survival threat to a misunderstanding
8. Blacks will be perceived as sounding and behaving aggressively more often	8. Black will invoke a language and style that may seem hostile and aggressive to an outsider
9. Loud voice and mannerism will be interpreted as aggressive and inappropriate	9. Loud voice and mannerism will be interpreted as normal and appropriate
10. Threat in aggressive situation is to call into action social and governmental forces	10. Threat in aggressive situation is to apply black community pressure and ostracism

ASSERTIVE BLACK MESSAGES

It is clear from the above that there is a high likelihood that what the black person perceives as an assertive message may be heard as an aggressive statement by a white recipient, because of references made to race. Therefore, if a black person is to communicate in an assertive and effective manner, there must be some thought given to the message or communication as it "fits" the receiver or target person. This means that black communicators must be aware of the various audiences they address in daily living — and the manner in which they may speak assertively but differently to members of each group. And again the "fit" or "matching" of the assertive message is important to the degree to which the black person sees it directly affecting his or her current or future survival. Among the various audiences that represent targets for an assertive message there are as many types as there are people, but four general categories can be identified:

1. Very conventional whites with middle class orientation
2. Non-conventional whites with mixed orientation
3. Blacks with middle class orientation
4. Blacks with black masses orientation

As one can easily see, an assertive message directed to category 4 (black masses) may have to be quite different from an assertive comment to category 1 (conventional white). For example, if a black student wanted a few members of category 1 to leave his room he might appropriately say, "Look fellahs, it has been nice having you visit, but I would appreciate you leaving since I must study." While that same black student faced with visitors representing category 4 could just as appropriately say, "Why don't you niggers get out of my room and go fuck around someplace else?" For the black student to be so ethnic with conventional whites (especially if his voice was loud) would stamp him as aggressive. But for his fellow blacks he would be assertive. The student may also choose the latter way of expressing himself so that he does not "sound white."

This dialogue demonstrates that assertive training from a black perspective must also recognize that the black communicator should be able to intentionally and consciously select the most appropriate assertive message considering the different types of people to be dealt with. Thus, considering the various audiences that black people have

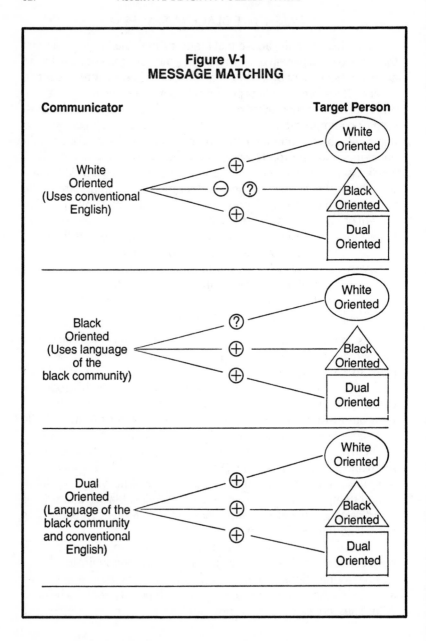

Figure V-1
MESSAGE MATCHING

as target groups and the varying degrees of importance these people represent, it is important to be concerned with the technique I call "Message Matching." (See Figure V-1). It may be seen from the figure that message matching is the process of considering various verbal options with regard to a target person and then selecting the most appropriate and effective assertive message.

Message matching is directly related to one's survival ladder. The survival ladder is the way people are divided in a person's mind in terms of the degree of control they have over the attainment of specific goals. (See Chapter VI) Message matching and survival ladder are just handy terms that describe what I am actually doing when working with a black client in assertive training. Let us take an example from my work with a black college student:

Me: Explain to me the hassle you're having with your teacher.

Client: It's the same old crap. I try to ask a question in class or see the dude after the class, and he ain't never got time. So I said later for that — and now he wants to fail me.

Me: Did you ever really take the time to rap with the teacher?

Client: Yeah.

Me: Exactly what did you say?

Client: I said, "Hey man, I want to talk to you about this paper." He said, "Have you read my comments?" I said, "Yeah, they don't make sense." And then he said somethun about, he didn't want to discuss it then so I should make an appointment. So I said, "Ah man, forget it!"

Me: I don't blame the teacher.

Client: What do you mean — now where are you comin from?

Me: Well, you kinda challenged the dude — you know — like confronted him with the paper and demanded that he talk to you then.

Client: No, man, it wasn't like that — I just walked up to the dude and ran down how I felt — he's kinda flakey anyhow.

Me: Do you need to pass the course?

Client: Yea, but I ain't going to kiss his ass.

Me: Suppose you were working on a job you really needed, and your boss had written down some comments on how to improve your performance — would you talk to him the same way you talked to your teacher?

Client: (long pause) No, I guess not.

Me: Why not?

Client: Well, if I needed the bread — well, I would hit on the dude just right.

Me: What would you say?

Client: Something like, I'd like to discuss those suggestions you wrote down (smile).

Me: Why did you smile?

Client: Sounded kinda funny — you know.

Me: Sounded white — like you were Tomin or something.

Client: Dig it — that's it.

Me: Did you have any of your partners with you when you spoke to your teacher?

Client: Yea — you know Freddy and Jo-Jo.

Me: And you had to maintain in front of them too.

Client: (Smile) — I don't know, you know — I really don't know.

Me: You have your choice as to how to let your teacher know your real feelings. You can come on strong — like you did — or you can clean up your act and deal with him on a different level. Those cats don't change, man, and some of them are threatened just because you are big and black — so why don't you be cool? And you don't have to have your partners around — just in case you're tempted to showboat. O.K.?

Client: Yeah I dig. (pause) If I really want the grade, then I best make a better impression — on the man's terms.

Me: Well, I would rather say, there are times when it will pay you to communicate in ways that the "man" understands. That means using standard English and all the things he considers appropriate in getting your point across. That doesn't mean you give up talking your talk to the brothers and sisters — it just means you are bilingual — and that you know when and where to use it.

Client: That's pretty hip. Like I've been diggin on you doing it too.

Me: (Smile) Yeah. That's the dues you pay when you live in two worlds — one black and one white.

WILL THE ASSERTIVE MESSAGE FIT?

Several things take place in the dialogue that was just described. There is first the attempt to work out the assertive message that best fits the target person (Message Matching). This procedure began with locating the target person (teacher who happens to be white) in the client's order of importance of people who control his/her "making it" (Survival Ladder). The survival ladder concept is also a convenient diagnostic tool that will both remind the facilitator to be sensitive to whom the black client has in mind as a target person and to work out the most effective assertive message to fit the situation.

This approach is to be used in a flexible manner to keep the facilitator alerted to the perceptions and priorities of the black client. The survival ladder questions are meant to tap the client's own choices of which people (out of all those who must be dealt with) to become assertive with, as well as which one to become less passive or less aggressive with. The implication here is that blacks may have to reconsider previous modes or habits of communication that were either predominantly passive or aggressive — but never assertive. The approach I demonstrate above is basically aimed at getting to the reality of the black experience in which a black person must live in a society and deal with people (frequently white) who cause him or her a great deal of anxiety. Because of the many pressures on a black person already discussed (e.g. Jim Crow Halo Effect, repressed hostility and anger, paranoia, and differences in style and use of language) there is difficulty in finding the assertive manner of expressing oneself that is both comfortable (not giving up one's black dignity and pride) and effective (manages to get the message across without *undue* harm). The usual black response in a state of anxiety has either been passive or aggressive — either say nothing or become loud, threatening and abusive. For whites, but particularly for blacks, assertiveness is a social skill. It can open the door for many who occasionally need or want to "play the game." This doesn't mean that they must "sell out," act white or become a "handkerchief head." It means increasing choice and options in terms of ways of communicating honest feelings. It increases the repertoire of responses and makes one less subject to exploitation. And, as the survival ladder may indicate, it not only pertains to relating with whites. Blacks have problems getting out of the "either-or" bag (either passive or aggressive) with friends, parents, in-laws, and neighbors. Assertiveness from a black perspective should deal with "what to say," and "how you say it" considering who one is talking to. Let us take an example of assertive training in a mental hospital setting:

Therapist: I understand you have trouble rapping with sisters (black women).

Patient: (Black Male) Yeah, that's right. I can seem to talk with white women, but I can't seem to get across to sisters. Like at the last social we had — there was this fine number I wanted to rap with — you know — just to get to know her — but I just didn't know how to go about it.

Therapist: What if the woman was white?

Patient: Well I would put on my gentleman act and break it on down.

Therapist: And with a sister...

Patient: Well, I'd either just go along with the program or cuss her ass out.

Therapist: O.K. — then maybe you're satisfied with that approach.

Patient: No — that's not the way it should be. I've got feelings and ideas that I really would like to get across — but I don't want her laughin at me or thinking I'm queer or square — you dig?

Here the black patient is anxious about being himself towards a black woman for fear of being considered "queer" or "square." In the same way he may fear expressing his love for his children or for his close friends. In almost all of these situations, the black person may be inhibited from expressing a sincere positive feeling (acting normal) because of some fear or anxiety. He may be unable to speak to authority figures for fear of "saying the wrong thing" and being considered a trouble maker; unable to give up hanging with his partners and studying for fear of being seen as "putting them down;" unable to speak up in a class or group for fear of acting "too smart" or asking a "stupid question." These interpersonal anxiety responses are the proper subject for assertive training from a black perspective — but it is essential that the facilitator know *who* that "someone" is as a target person and *what* that person represents in the eyes of the black client. In this sense a very important practice differing with conventional approaches may be necessary with black clients: one should begin assertive training where the client's level of inhibition is the highest. In this view I disagree with Salter, the pioneer of assertive techniques, as quoted by Wolpe, "Therapy should begin where the patient's level of inhibition is lowest." (Wolpe, 1969).

This difference of approach reflects the contrasting attitudes between whites and backs as to what effective treatment entails. In my experience, most blacks have little time (or money) to "fool around," desire to get right to the point, want their most pressing concerns dealt with and expect to benefit from directness and specific suggestions. Recent research indicates the relative dissatisfaction of blacks compared to whites with their experiences with treatment facilities and the black's preference for black therapists. (Wolkon, Moriwaki and Williams 1973). As I already indicated, their self disclosure is low and "paranoia" is high. As Harper and Stone (1974) have noted: "...if the counselor is to be effective with Blacks, it is suggested that he orient himself to techniques that will quickly bring the black counselee to a level of awareness and action. In other words, the counselor must be directive, confrontive, and persuasive in getting his counselee to be rational and active. Many blacks do not have the patience and time for the passive and slow therapies; often their concerns and problems demand immediate action."

I also concur with Harper and Stone when they point out that the masses of black people have experienced failure in the system, which necessitates a departure from a slow approach with long-range results. For these reasons, when counseling blacks it may be best to modify and/or reverse many conventional ideas in assertive training (please see *Publisher's Note*, Appendix II).

THE INTENTION AND THE MESSAGE — A DIDACTIC APPROACH

Assertive behavior training from a black perspective requires that we deal with a basic problem in human communication. It is generally agreed that there are three parts to the process of communicating — the person communicating (sender), the communication itself (message) and the receiver of the message (target person). It is often assumed that the intention of the communicator or sender is correctly perceived and received by the target person. In other words, it may be assumed that if the sender of a message *intends* for the message to be assertive it is *received* as assertive; *intends* for the message to be aggressive, it is *received* as aggressive. We all know, however, that our intentions are frequently misunderstood (along with our messages) and there is a higher chance of this happening with people who do not share the same cultural definitions, as may happen between blacks and whites.

Figure V-2

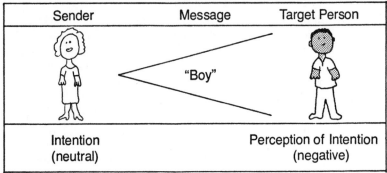

Sender	Message	Target Person
	"Boy"	
Intention (neutral)		Perception of Intention (negative)

A perfect example of this cultural gap is the use of the word "boy" by a white person toward someone black. The white "sender" may intend no harm, while the black "target" hears the message as aggressive and interprets it as a "put down." In this same manner, white business organizations that train their company representatives to use the first names of their customers are in conflict with black perceptions that see this as a way of not showing respect by avoiding the use of "Mr." or "Mrs.," or titles of respect such as "Rev." and "Dr." Thus, the question assertive training must deal with is "are there some real differences in the way blacks and whites may perceive the same message?" My experience indicates that the answer is yes.

"Hey boy, would you mind getting in line like the rest of us?" may be intended as assertive by a white but is heard as aggressive by a black. In the same way a white attempting to join a black group in conversation is seen as putting them down by saying "Can I come over and join you people?" Among many blacks, "you people" is a put down phrase. In a like manner, the comments of many blacks which may be intended as assertive may be perceived as aggressive by whites, because of the use of certain words, voice tone, body posturing or gestures. Frequently doctors and other professionals have told me about a black patient's "hostile" walk, "menacing" look or "threatening" air — non-verbal communication that may be passive or assertive but which is perceived as aggressive.

If this problem exists (and there is considerable evidence that it does) then an additional didactic factor must be introduced into assertive behavior training for blacks that recognizes this ethnic subtlety. I say "for blacks" because frequently, in communicating with whites who represent some form of power, blacks may be penalized for communications (messages) that are seen as aggressive. The problem exists for *anyone* who attempts to be assertive with someone in power, but the "survival" factor is greater for blacks, as has been shown. Assertive training should provide blacks with options for expressing feelings along with the knowledge of how those expressions may be perceived by traditional whites or judgmental blacks. (This is also known as how to "play the game").

The problem is that the black client may intend to be assertive and would be considered assertive by a black target person but aggressive by a white target person. So what do we do with the issue of the *intentions* of the communicator being misperceived by the target person? Who really decides if the message is assertive, passive or aggressive — the sender or the receiver? It is fine when both agree — but what if they don't? This is where the facilitator must be sufficiently skilled and sensitive to know or find out the intention of the client's message. The client should be told about the various perceptions that can be formed from the message, depending upon whether one is listening with a white or black ear. This type of feedback lets the client know how different standards may be applied to him/her — sometimes without his/her knowledge and to his/her detriment. The didactic presentation of this added dimension in communication helps the client to understand and develop responses that "white oriented" audiences would consider appropriate.

helps the client to understand and develop responses that "white oriented" audiences would consider appropriate.

Having this type of knowledge allows the client to be truly bilingual in assertive communications — to "talk black" when and where it is fitting, and to "talk white" when they need to protect themselves from harm or penalizing judgments. It is good sense to defend oneself by being familiar with the communication system that can be used against you.

This problem of intentions matching perceptions may have different dimensions for those blacks who already fluently "talk white." Through education, employment or association, many blacks are comfortable with standard white expressions. They are frequently referred to as middle class, although the term has a different meaning for whites in comparison to blacks. At any rate, the difficulty of using standard white communications may be less a problem for this group. Of course, there are those blacks who are somewhat unfamiliar with, or look down upon black-oriented terms and styles of expression. They are like the blacks observed by Frantz Fanon (1967): "to the extent the subjugated colonial can adopt the mother country's cultural standards, he becomes whiter and renounces his blackness." These are the blacks who feel that a large part of traditional black communication is crude, common and essentially street talk. They, like many whites, would benefit from this didactic aspect of assertive behavior training that reflects upon the value of being able to assert oneself (and accept another's assertiveness) as one really feels it and can best express it.

Many of us with an African heritage have had our minds "white washed" by consistent exposure to white education, white values and white standards. For the black population which feels distant from certain cultural expressions, it may be helpful to consider the original function of black language. As Jim Haskins and Hugh Butts (1973) point out, "One may consider verbal behavior in blacks as serving several functions: (1) as a defense against individualized and institutional racist behavior in whites, (2) as an aspect of the black lifestyle reflecting healthy group narcissism, cohesive bonds, and affection; (3) as an avenue for the release of rage, fear, guilt, and other affects on an individual basis." This idea of expressing oneself honestly to whites — as far as blacks are concerned, is an area filled with problems primarily the white standards of what is "appropriate" communication. Whites seem to like lots of "pleases," "pardon me's," "if it's all right's," "nice" language and indirectness in their communications. Blacks when they are not passive seem to be much more direct, impatient with evasiveness and resistant to long discussion. Haskins and Butts (1973) observe that "Black verbal expression, on the other hand, tends to be much more direct, with no interposition between subject and object. It is such directness that characterizes the black experience."

An example of black directness is presented by a black employee requesting a day off:

Employee: How bout gettin tomorrow off — I gotta take care of a little business.

Supervisor: Well, William, we are short-handed and we are running behind in production.

Employee: Look, man, I didn't ask you about how many hands you got and all that — I'm just talking about the day off — you know — like just tell me if I can get the day off.

Supervisor: Now look, William, I have other responsibilities and have to take your request into consideration.

Employee: Wow, man, like you just can't even answer a question — just one simple question and we have to go all through these changes.

The directness of the employee's request (without any niceties thrown in) and the perceived confrontive tone that the question be answered immediately is frequently alarming to whites. This for the black employee may be assertive but a white supervisor (or group facilitator) may perceive it differently. There are ready-made words for assertive blacks — impudent, impolite, arrogant, hostile, aggressive and abrasive. I have personally been called most of these for behavior that my wife and I agreed was merely "expressing my feelings without putting anyone down." It was at those times that I wished a replay was possible and I could have really showed them what an aggressive black message was all about. Then they would have had a frame of reference for comparing an assertive statement to an aggressive one!

FOOTNOTES

[20] Andrews, M. and Owens, P.T., *Black Language*. Los Angeles: Seymour-Smith, ©1973, p. 26. Used by permission.

[21] Haskins, J. and Butts, H.F., *The Psychology of Black Language*. N.Y.: Harper & Row, ©1973, p. 60. Used by permission.

[22] Andrews, M. and Owens, P.T., op. cit., p. 16. Used by permission.

CHAPTER VI

Techniques from a Black Perspective

"One of the most common
approaches social scientists make to
the study of the Negro experience in
this country is to draw up a
questionnaire based on the white
experience . . . When they find that
the response patterns of the Negro
differ significantly from those of the
whites, they conclude that the Negro
responses are deviant and need to be
explained."
Andrew Billingsley
Black Families in White America

TOOLS FOR ASSERTIVE TRAINING

Reference has been made in earlier chapters to inventories and questionnaires that can function as aids in the initial steps of assertive behavior training from a black perspective. In order to guide the focus of the facilitator and at the same time gain insight into the black client's perceptions, I suggest the use of the following tools which I have developed for use in my own counseling, consulting, and work with graduate students:

1) The Assertive Inventory
2) The Survival Ladder
3) A Black-White Language Questionnaire
4) The "Before You Work With Blacks" Test
5) A Group Awareness Profile (GAP Test)

Each of these aids is geared to provide the practitioner with some rough parameters and basic information that can be used to shed light on the black-white implications of assertiveness. These assertive training aids are not standardized research instruments that have benefited from scaling procedures or statistical tests of significance. They merely provide responses that can be used for individual comparisons within a group or impressionistic interpretation by the facilitator. Nevertheless, such responses can be valuable in helping the client objectively look at himself or herself while providing a concrete beginning point for both the client and the facilitator. Let's examine each tool separately:

1) The Assertive Inventory

The twenty questions I have included in this inventory are meant to provide a good beginning diagnosis. The number of "yeses" can immediately provide a rough picture of the extent to which the respondent needs help in being assertive. The particular problems to which the client answers "yes" can provide specific areas for the therapist to focus upon and later use for practice. Answers to the last four questions (#17, #18, #19 and #20) provide insight into how the client has been socialized and influenced by parents, teachers or others. These questions are developed to provide cues as to how much time may need to be spent in re-orienting the client and preparing him or her to appreciate the value of assertiveness.

Particular attention to several of the items of the Inventory (#2, #7, #8, #9, #10, #12, #16, #18, #19) will assist the therapist to determine the extent to which *anxiety* is a major factor limiting the client's assertiveness. If the answer to nearly all of these items is "yes," the facilitator may wish to examine the anxiety factor in greater depth.

In addition to the importance of the survival oriented inhibitions created by the black experience in a white dominant society, it is also true that anxiety itself may be a very powerful inhibitor of the development of assertion. Fear of possible consequences, fear of the attention of others, and other anxieties may not be dissipated by skills training alone. The alert and responsible facilitator must be aware of the effects of anxiety and see that the appropriate treatment takes place, in addition to any assertiveness training. This may be particularly true with respect to black clients who have traditionally been conditioned to "fake it" rather than reveal personal inadequacies. Now they are being encouraged to reveal their anxieties and the situation itself may be extremely threatening to them. They may know what they want to achieve, but find that they "freeze" when confronted with the situation. With such clients, it is important for the counselor to avoid suggesting steps of developing assertiveness.

The counselor should pay attention to the clues that anxiety is at a high level (e.g., chronic nervous mannerisms, persistent reluctance to initiate assertive acts, self-reported fears), and employ techniques to reduce the level. Humor and/or music may be effective means to reduce anxiety in such situations, however more severe anxiety levels

THE ASSERTIVE INVENTORY

1.	I would hesitate to write a complaining letter to a business or company.	yes	no	not sure
2.	At times I want to say things but I don't.	yes	no	not sure
3.	I hesitate to take things back to the store.	yes	no	not sure
4.	I get convinced to do things that I don't want to do.	yes	no	not sure
5.	I would find it hard to tell someone near me to stop smoking.	yes	no	not sure
6.	It is difficult for me to ask my friends for help.	yes	no	not sure
7.	I spend a lot of time avoiding conflicts.	yes	no	not sure
8.	I find it difficult to openly express love and affection.	yes	no	not sure
9.	I find it hard to tell people no.	yes	no	not sure
10.	I frequently have opinions that I don't express.	yes	no	not sure
11.	I find it hard to disagree with people close to me.	yes	no	not sure
12.	I hesitate to speak up in a group discussion or argument.	yes	no	not sure
13.	When I plan to be busy, people can keep me from doing things.	yes	no	not sure
14.	I usually would rather go along with someone I don't really know rather than to have a disagreement or argument.	yes	no	not sure
15.	I usually have to get angry before I say what I want to say.	yes	no	not sure
16.	I have a lot of concern about expressing myself and hurting someone's feelings.	yes	no	not sure
17.	I have been taught it is not right to raise your voice or risk hurting someone's feelings.	yes	no	not sure
18.	I consider it wise to avoid arguments.	yes	no	not sure
19.	I believe that people should keep their angry feelings to themselves.	yes	no	not sure
20.	Being liked is very important to me.	yes	no	not sure

will require appropriate clinical interventions, such as systematic desensitization (Wolpe, 1969; Fensterheim, 1975). If responses to the Assertive Inventory and other client cues create some doubt regarding the presence of excessive anxiety, the counselor may wish to use some form of systematic assessment, such as the Willoughby Schedule (Wolpe, 1969) or the self-report "Subjective Units of Disturbance Scale" (Cotler and Guerra, 1976).

2) The Survival Ladder

This chart has a two-fold purpose. First, I use it to help the client to think of the different "somebodys" that they would like to be assertive with (either past, present or future). Second, I use it to locate the place of the client's "Target Person" in relationship to the client's perception of survival or of "making it." With good insight one researcher correctly observes,

> In the ghetto there is consensus that the problem of every individual is 'making it'; 'How you makin it, man?' is a common form of greeting. Interviews I have conducted in the black community suggest that 'making it with dignity' is central to a leading concept of manhood. (Blauner, 1970)

While it is important for the facilitator to be sensitive to the survival ladder of any person in assertive training, for the black client it is *crucial*. The survival ladder is the placing of people (or groups) in orderly steps according to the degrees to which they represent a major factor in the client "making it." The usual range is 1 to 7, from the least external control over the client's goals (represented by level 1) to the most external control (represented by level 7). Usually there is a corresponding increase in stress attached to delivery of the assertive message as one goes from 1 to 7. Of course the order may change for any particular individual. I especially urge the counselor to identify specific examples of problems that relate more closely to the client's reality than the samples I have given. The implication of such a mental classification and message matching system has been stated by many investigators. Wolpe has noted,

> We find patients who are able to competently handle tradesmen and strangers, but are timorous and submissive with anybody important like a mother, a wife, or a lover — or to only one of these. By contrast, there are those who dominate (and occasionally tyrannize) over close associates, but are fearful ... with the outgroup. (Wolpe, 1969).

SURVIVAL LADDER

Levels of Survival and Degree of External Control	Roles as Targets for Assertive Behavior Skills	Sample Problems
1. Daily Routine	bus driver-passenger	-passenger offering me tickets/asking about luggage
	waiter-customer	-being seated next to kitchen
		-spotted wine glass
	salesclerk-customer	-states price, inferring black's inability to pay
	bank clerk	-inferior services to blacks
	telephone operator	
	bartender	
	secretaries (different when secretary is black or white)	
	taxi	-overcharging
	train, airline, bus	-passenger telling another about smoking

Levels of Survival and Degree of External Control	Roles as Targets for Assertive Behavior Skills	Sample Problems
2. Leisure/Recreation	peers-friends parties rap sessions picnics	-not eating certain foods -being a vegetarian -smoking
3. Home	parent-child husband-wife spouse-friends spouse-in-laws siblings-brother siblings-sister relatives-grandparents uncles, etc.	-not smoking in home -sexual relationships -household tasks -who gets educational support -stealing ash trays in front of children while dining out.
4. Community Involvement	neighbors, church clubs, committees schools (as parents) clergy-parishioner	-collections for causes you disagree with -community services not made available to blacks -non-drinker refusing drink from white authority figure

5. School/Educational	student-student teacher-administrator student-teacher student-administrator	-BSU pressure on black student -unfair white teacher in English
6. Job/Profession	supervisor-supervisee employer-employee maid-boss	-male wearing braided hair -white boss wanting to be "fixed up" with black woman -white secretaries that don't send you memos -secretaries who will not address professional black by title
7. Aging/Institutionalization	wards-correctional officer probationer-probation officer social worker-client (special groups) Aged: stigma, physically handicapped, blind/deaf/ dumb/crippled Institutionalized: (hospital, juvenile hall) patient ward male-female	-others sneezing or coughing in your direction -denial of rights by institution

3) A Black-White Language Questionnaire

This questionnaire also has a two-fold purpose. First it seeks to sensitize the client that two modes of communication do exist and may be the occasional reason for a lack of understanding between two people. Second, it tries to determine which mode of expression is most comfortable to and preferred by the client. Three distinct preferential styles should emerge; the black client who is more at home talking black than white; the black client who prefers to talk white rather than black, and the black person who is equally at ease with either black or white modes of communication. The implications for the therapist are obvious — the degree to which the facilitator is dual-oriented and capable of dialogue in black or white terms may determine the extent to which meaningful communication takes place.

BLACK-WHITE LANGUAGE QUESTIONNAIRE

Many blacks use expressions and ways of communicating or rapping that are part of living in the black community. In some way it may differ from the typical manner in which whites talk and express themselves in the white community. With that in mind please answer the following questions (circle the answer you feel most applies to you):

SECTION A	Not At All	Some-what	Very Much
I am familiar with black language.	5	3	1
I am comfortable with black language.	5	3	1
I use black language myself.	5	3	1
TOTAL SCORE SECTION A _____			

SECTION B			
I am familiar with white language.	5	3	1
I am comfortable with white language.	5	3	1
I use white language myself.	5	3	1
TOTAL SCORE SECTION B _____			

Scoring information on page 89.

---

4) The "Before You Work With Blacks" Test

These 34 questions are designed to provide a practitioner with a self-appraisal and self-analysis of readiness to work with black clients. There is no pass or fail but I do consider ten of the questions to be crucial. I suggest that the reader take the test at this point before reading further.

THE "BEFORE YOU WORK WITH BLACKS" TEST

	Very Much	Some- what	Not At All
1. Are you aware of the meaning of miscegenation for blacks?	☐	☐	☐
2. Are you familiar with black language?	☐	☐	☐
3. Are you aware of the way American blacks and West Indian blacks perceive each other?	☐	☐	☐
4. Are you familiar with the works of E. Franklin Frazier?	☐	☐	☐
5. Are you familiar with the book *Black Bourgeoisie?*	☐	☐	☐
6. Are you comfortable with black language?	☐	☐	☐
7. If female, do you understand the meaning of being "hit on?"	☐	☐	☐
8. Are you aware of what it means to "play to dozens?"	☐	☐	☐
9. Are the names and works of the following people familiar to you: Horace Cayton and St. Clair Drake?	☐	☐	☐
10. Do you use black language yourself?	☐	☐	☐
11. Are you familiar with the feeling blacks have about "Jim Crow?"	☐	☐	☐
12. Do you desire black supervision of your work with black clients?	☐	☐	☐

	Very Much	Some-what	Not At All
13. Do you really understand the meaning of "the Black Experience" as used by American blacks?	☐	☐	☐
14. Do you understand the difference in using the terms Negro, colored and Black?	☐	☐	☐
15. Are you comfortable with black style of "rapping" in terms of voice volume, facial gestures, hand movements and posturing?	☐	☐	☐
16. Are you comfortable with the use of the word "mothafucka?"	☐	☐	☐
17. Could you accept and encourage conversations about "the man," "whitey" or "Honkies?"	☐	☐	☐
18. As a parent, would you approve of your son or daughter dating an average (whatever you consider average) black youth?	☐	☐	☐
19. Would you seek out competent black consultation or supervision in working with different black patients?	☐	☐	☐
20. Are you familiar with the works of Frantz Fanon?	☐	☐	☐
21. Have you had exposure to professional training conducted by blacks (classes, workshops, seminars)?	☐	☐	☐
22. Have you been exposed to the professional views of black women as well as black men?	☐	☐	☐
23. Are you familiar with the current literature, journals and periodicals in which blacks express their professional views?	☐	☐	☐
24. Have you been involved in black-oriented meetings or caucuses of professional organizations like APA?	☐	☐	☐
25. Have you ever exposed *your approach to counseling blacks* to other blacks in the profession (as individuals or in a group) for a response (or advice)?	☐ ☐	☐ ☐	☐ ☐

	Very Much	Some-what	Not At All
26. Do you feel that, generally speaking, blacks can counsel blacks better than whites?	☐	☐	☐
27. Have you had specific formal training in dealing with ethnic minorities?	☐	☐	☐
28. Do you feel you have close black friends (not acquaintances) who give you an ongoing sensitivity of what it means to be black?	☐	☐	☐
29. Do you understand why many blacks would be passive with a white therapist but aggressive with fellow blacks?	☐	☐	☐
30. Are you familiar with the studies dealing with black self-revelation?	☐	☐	☐
31. Do you understand the term "Toming" as it describes a particular relationship between a black and a white?	☐	☐	☐
32. Have you ever lived in, worked in or been exposed to a ghetto in more than just a "visitor" capacity (eg. American Friends Service Committee projects)?	☐	☐	☐
33. Do you possess some intimate and personal experiences that allows you to have special insights into black lifestyles? (eg. interracial marriage, passing)	☐	☐	☐
34. Are you aware of what an oreo is?	☐	☐	☐

Many black professionals, including myself, would have serious reservations about the effectiveness with black clients of a therapist who marks "not at all" on one or more of 10 key questions. Those key questions are #6, #12, #17, #18, #19, #21, #22, #23, #25, and #27. In this sense a "not at all" response on any of those questions would amount to failing the test; the therapist is not yet "ready" to counsel blacks effectively. While no one can be completely ruled out on the basis of this questionnaire, the consensus opinion of the professional blacks that I have talked with is that a person wishing to counsel black clients is in deep trouble if he or she cannot answer "somewhat" or "very much" to 20 of the 34 questions: numbers 1, 2, 4, 6, 11, 12, 13, 14, 15, 17, 18, 19, 21, 22, 23, 25, 27, 29, 31 and 34. The questions that one could respond "not at all" to and still do an adequate job were numbers 3, 5, 7, 8, 9, 10, 16, 20, 24, 26, 28, 30, 32 and 33.

Even some blacks may not have a perfect score, which indicates that just being born a black does not automatically make one a therapist for blacks — but most blacks would score higher just from living the black experience. If the race designation is turned around and this questionnaire is used for those blacks desiring to counsel whites, we would expect answers automatically to be easier, since most of the exposure blacks have had has been to white views, literature, friends and lifestyles. The dominant group is always better known than the minority group. After responding to those questions, an individual should be aware of some minimal expectations for counseling black persons. There is no way, yet, of measuring the therapist's sincerity and dedication to the struggle of black people.

5) A Group Awareness Profile (GAP Test)

I use this diagnostic tool to bring attention to the different ways the respondent will think and act towards blacks in contrast to whites. The profile is helpful in understanding the extent to which the client will make distinctions between black and white "target persons." It also sensitizes both the client and the therapist to the racial component contained in assertive responses. Complete the GAP Test on page 86 before reading further.

Based on past experiences with varied black groups, I would suggest that if the client has six or more responses in the aggressive category, six or more in the *passive* category or six or more in the *not sure* category, then there is a definite problem and need for help in being assertive. Questions 7 and 8 will usually provide answers that indicate such a need. The answers to questions 9 and 12 also indicate a potential source of problems, especially if the two answers are not similar. Of course the ideal response is for the client to circle *assertive* for all 21 questions. The degree to which the client departs from this ideal response is an indication of the extent to which he or she may need assertive training.

The techniques presented in this chapter provide basic tools for the conduct of assertive behavior training with black clients. Potential assertive trainers are urged to examine carefully their own readiness ("Before You Work With Blacks"), and to offer services only when their skills and awareness are compatible with client needs.

GROUP AWARENESS PROFILE (GAP TEST)

	passive	assertive	aggressive	not sure
1. I think most whites would see *me* as	passive	assertive	aggressive	not sure
2. I think most blacks would see *me* as	passive	assertive	aggressive	not sure
3. I think most white people *are*	passive	assertive	aggressive	not sure
4. I think most black people *are*	passive	assertive	aggressive	not sure
5. I *would like* most white people to see me as	passive	assertive	aggressive	not sure
6. I *would like* most black people to see me as	passive	assertive	aggressive	not sure
7. I think I usually look	passive	assertive	aggressive	not sure
8. I think I usually act	passive	assertive	aggressive	not sure
9. With a black person it is easy for me to be	passive	assertive	aggressive	not sure
10. With a white person it is easy for me to be	passive	assertive	aggressive	not sure
11. With a black person it is hard for me to be	passive	assertive	aggressive	not sure
12. With a white person it is hard for me to be	passive	assertive	aggressive	not sure

CHAPTER VII

Guiding the Black Client to Effective Assertion

> " . . .I reacted by trying to be pleasant
> — it being a great part of the
> American Negro's education (long
> before he goes to school) that he must
> make people 'like' him."
> James Baldwin
> *Notes of a Native Son*

In looking at the many variables that can be considered, four key ideas emerge as those that should be placed into a program of assertive behavior training for blacks.

The *first* of these is to determine the degree to which black, in contrast with white, communication styles will play a part in spontaneous interaction. Let's look at the following example from a training group:

Client A: "Hey, man, (to another black client) get out of my seat."

Client B: "I didn't see your name on it."

Client A: "Man, if you don't move your behind out of that chair —"

Client B: "Yeah? You gonna move me?"

Client A: "You want me to put a hurtin on you?"

Therapist: "Wait a minute — just a minute. We can't have anything like that in here."

Client A: (Turning around) "What's wrong with you?"

Therapist: "I'm just saying we can't have any rough stuff."

(Client A and Client B look at each other with puzzled expressions.)

Client A: "Rough stuff?" (In a quizical voice).

Therapist: "That's right, that's right. You two boys were getting ready to get involved."

Client B: "Boys? Involved? Man, who the fuck you callin boys — I mean lets clear that up. (Turns to Client A with outstretched hand and Client B slaps his palm.) I mean, we just talkin to each other and you come with all that off the wall "boy" shit. That ain't cool — that ain't cool at all."

Therapist: "Well, obviously I thought that one person was going to make trouble for the other over the chair."

Client A and B: (Smiling at each other.)

Client B: "That's no big thing. We always talk like that to each other. You sure jump to a lot of conclusions quick."

Therapist: "I guess so; can we talk after this session?"
Client A: "Yeah, I guess so."

The black communication style known as "sounding" or "woofin" was obviously a problem for the facilitator to interpret properly. This provides a cue to all involved that black in-group expressions can be very difficult for an unaware white to correctly interpret.

A *second* factor is to establish the intent of the message, as perceived by the client (since by white standards it may appear to be aggressive or passive). An example of this may be seen in the following situation:

Facilitator: "Any comments about our session?"
Client: "I didn't appreciate the way you sounded on me about being late for the group meeting."
Facilitator: "I wasn't just singling you out; I was making it a general comment."
Client: "That was no general comment, man, you were looking dead at me when you started that crap about people being late and what does that mean to the group."
Facilitator: "I don't know why you should take it personally and get hostile about it."
Client: (Voice rising) "Hey man, I'm not hostile — you asked for comments didn't you? You know, like it seems to me that you're the one that's gettin upset. You ask a question and then don't want to hear nothin."
Facilitator: "Well, go right ahead with your comments."
Client: "No man, you go right ahead and run things like you've been doing."

The immediate assumption that the client was being hostile may have been based on the white facilitator's standards of "appropriate" conversation. The loud or raised voice and use of "street talk" often places professionals on the defensive. Most should check first by simply asking, "Are you angry?" or "Are you feeling hostile?" instead of quickly making the assumption that the message contains anger or hostility.

Third, the facilitator should be aware of the type of target person to whom the message is directed and be prepared to judge the "matching" or "fitting" quality (e.g., street peer vs. supervisor).

The *fourth* and last point is to provide a frame of reference for comparing the assertive message by having the client express it in the other modes of passive and aggressive speech.

Additional information with regard to the preference for black or white communication style may be obtained by a facilitator through the use of the short "Black-White Language Questionnaire" already presented and discussed in Chapter VI.

The comparative scores from the two sections provide a rough indication of the degree to which the respondent is balanced in orientation or leans toward the black or white style of communicating. Three ideal types emerge from this comparison of columns: 1) The predominately *black-oriented* language type (scoring 15 in Section A and 5 or less in Section B) who would offer the biggest challenge to the white "traditional" assertive behavior trainer; 2) The *dual-oriented* type (scoring 9 or 15 in Section A and 9 or 15 in Section B) who would usually go along (and play the game) with the facilitator; and 3) the predominately *white-oriented* language type (scoring 5 or less in Section A and 15 in Section B) who, if black, may tend to have questions about black language styles and be most comfortable for a white-oriented therapist to work with.

A major test for an assertive training program is its effectiveness in assisting clients of the two extreme styles to be aware of the "match" and "fit" of their assertive messages with respect to black and white targets. This should take place while at the same time developing the assertive skills of the dual-oriented person.

CHAPTER VIII

Assertive Guidelines From a Black Perspective

> "We have been passive and
> accommodating through so many
> years of your insults and delays that
> you think the way things used to be is
> normal."
> Shirley Chisholm
> *Unbought and Unbossed*

A BLACK ASSERTIVE BEHAVIOR TRAINING PROGRAM

At this point let us pull together and discuss the major factors necessary to apply assertive behavior training from a black perspective. Figure VIII-1 shows how the basic approach can be visualized. It's almost like imagining a building — first, the foundation consists of five major points that provide the basic underpinnings (The most important at the bottom and the rest flow upward). Then each step is built on the foundation, the first five steps being the items of preparation discussed in Chapters II-VII, and the next five being geared into action. The major differences between conventional assertive training and an approach from a black perspective can easily be noted.

First, the foundation calls for a form of awareness and understanding that is not part of the traditional education or training of professional "helpers." Second, the area devoted to preparation is a little more time consuming and extensive than would be the occasion for white clients, due to the resistance that most blacks feel about self revelation. This longer period of preparation also deals with the "cultural paranoia" of blacks and the lack of real commitment towards therapy or counseling, in contrast to white clients who tend to more readily accept treatment.

The preparation period also provides for blacks an opportunity to "check out" the facilitator or therapist to find out just where he or she is coming from. This is extremely important since the willingness to risk exposing oneself, to participate in role playing or to really use the facilitator as a model will depend upon the degree to which the black client considers the facilitator "legitimate." Basic rapport, confidence and "good vibes" are developed during the preparation period. As the reader will see in the description of assertive group meetings, extra

Figure VIII-1

STRUCTURE OF A BLACK ASSERTIVE BEHAVIOR TRAINING PROGRAM

Action	10	Offer feedback and support; encourage client to try it some more, based upon feedback.
	9	Encourage person to go out and try it; discuss accepting assertions of others.
	8	Conduct practice sessions (target modeling, rehearsals, feedback, typical problems)
	7	Go over the basic elements of assertion (target, message, intent, components)
	6	Relate assertiveness and reaction to music (use 7 basic questions)
Preparation	5	Discuss social reality of black-black and black-white assertiveness (use GAP) (Jim Crow Halo effect and psycho-historical background)
	4	Discuss being assertive, aggressive or passive and the black person's background ("Before You Work With Blacks")
	3	Determine tendency to use black, white or dual-oriented language (use Black-White language Questionnaire)
	2	Obtain description, especially racial, of the "somebody" the client wants to be assertive with (use Survival Ladder)
	1	Introduce and explain assertive training as something most people can benefit from; assess anxiety level of client (use Assertive Inventory)
Foundation		• Understand implications of target person being black oriented, white oriented or dual oriented.
		• Be sensitive to racial variation in perceptions of appropriateness and language.
		• Be aware of the psycho-historical background of blacks.
		• Remember 10 characteristics of Jim Crow Halo Effect.
		• Evaluate your own readiness to work with blacks (use "Before You Work With Blacks" test)

time is devoted to answering "unasked" questions in the effort to make everyone comfortable. Blacks are very astute at "playing it cool" in new or threatening situations. So even though they have their "front" together the facilitator has to be sensitive and aware enough to deal with the unexpressed doubts and anxieties.

The action phase begins by taking private feelings and translating them into public expression. Music is used as a natural and familiar medium to facilitate this process. It also allows the client to get in contact with the feeling or affective level of what assertion is all about. Here the person gets the feeling of assertiveness: open, spontaneous, positive self-expression. Gospel music is used since it represents a traditional area of identification for blacks — it communicates a message, honestly expresses an emotional feeling and has no intention of putting anyone down. For blacks, it is the perfect model of assertiveness — it clearly tells it like it is with no fear of hurting anyone's feelings. But more important, in talking about publicly dropping one's inhibitions, music is generally a comfortable guide for grasping the feeling of spontaneous expression. People whistle, sing, dance, pop their fingers and move their bodies to music — even those who resist expressing themselves in other ways. To capture this type of spontaneity (or at least to examine it) and to apply the principles of this uninhibited behavior to assertive training is a major goal in working with black clients. "Let's get that partyin energy used for some constructive purposes" is a different way of stating the case. "Folks who can dance and do their thang all night, sure should have no problems being assertive" also sums up the objective. The major idea is to use the black person's reaction to music as a point of departure. This leads to examining the behavioral reactions on a conscious level and to trying out new types of assertive expression. Spontaneous reaction to music can keep the idea of assertiveness from being something new, foreign and "white." Of course, if the person has no reaction to the music, his or her inability to relate to a rhythmic beat should be accepted and examined. There may be fears or anxieties that need more intensive individual attention. Or the person may just not be in the mood to respond. For a young person there may be the need to share with the facilitator the type of music to which they can relate. This means bringing a selection of their own choosing to the individual or group session. Of course this underscores the reality that the response to Gospel music by blacks will be as varied as there are social, political, regional and age differences. Even without development of unexpressed feeling or an outward response, the general idea is usually acceptable, at least as an example of how other people express themselves assertively through music.

Many therapists may want to skip the idea of using music as a stimulus. Some will feel awkward in using a technique that is not traditionally part of working with people in therapy. Others will imagine that finding the right music, getting a tape recording or setting up a record player will be just too much trouble. Such problems may provide more insight into the therapist than into the client. If this area is passed over because of real equipment problems, the ideas already touched upon can still be useful in discussing the basic elements of assertion: spontaneity of expression along with honestly and openly communicating one's feelings.

The remaining action phase concentrates on understanding the basic elements of assertion, practice sessions and actual trials in real life. Again, differing from assertive training guidelines offered by others, I emphasize target person sensitivity (anticipating that some interaction may vary on the basis of racial and other variables); intent of the message (being the ultimate judge of one's own assertion); and content of message (discussing various cultural and racial styles that help to define the word "appropriate"). Time is also spent in dealing with acceptance of the assertive behavior of others.

SHORT CUT ASSERTIVE BEHAVIOR TRAINING

What should you do, if you have only a brief or restricted opportunity to apply assertive training? What if you have time limits, meeting space and equipment problems? What are the most essential elements of the approach that I propose?

For those who may have to function under a variety of such handicaps we should look at a skeleton assertive training program — the bare bones with no meat. Considered in this way, steps 1, 5, 7 and 8 would represent a *minimum* exposure. The therapist would simply introduce the general need for assertive training (using the the the assertive inventory), discuss the social realities of interracial assertiveness (using the GAP inventory), go over the basic elements of assertion and conduct some practice sessions. Of course, this all assumes that the facilitator has prepared by acquiring the basic foundation previously discussed.

This abbreviated approach is better than no training at all for individual clients but I do not advise it for use with groups. As can be seen, it leaves out an adequate preparation period, and provides minimal opportunity for "real life" experimenting and feedback.

LET'S PUT IT INTO ACTION — A STEP-BY-STEP GUIDE FOR A BLACK A-T GROUP

Keeping in mind the 10 basic steps that make up assertive preparation and action, it is time to see how these ideas can be put into practice. Since that is most easily accomplished by presenting an example, let's "tune in" on a "typical" assertive training group composed of black young adults.

Session 1

(Group of seven black young adults.)
After they are seated and have introduced themselves:
Step I:
Me: This is an assertive training group. No one should feel there is anything "wrong" with being in assertive training. All of us — myself included — have at times allowed people to take advantage of us — run us over — do us in. There have been times when all of us have faced occasions or situations where we should have spoken up — said what we wanted to say — as some of the books would say, stood up, and talked back. In fact, let's check on my first assumption. How many in here can look back in their past and think of some situations in which they wish they had spoken up but didn't? — Or wished they had expressed themselves honestly and directly — you know, just plain stood up for themselves — how many? Raise your hands. (Hands raised). As you see, all of us are in the same boat. We all feel there were times we should have asserted ourselves but didn't. Why didn't

we assert ourselves in those past situations? Can anyone here guess some of the reasons people don't say what they really want to say?

John: Sometimes you don't want to hurt someone's feelings.

Mary: You may not really be sure how somebody is going to take it.

Alex: It may be somebody important and you need to stay on their good side.

Paula: Sometimes you get so mad you don't trust yourself as to how it's going to come out.

Alma: Yeah, I know one time I was getting ready to straighten this teacher out, and while I was gonna do my thang when I just caught myself and said later — I ain't gonna say nuthin to this dude.

Bertha: Yeah, I remember one time I was with my mother and this bus driver wouldn't take our transfer tickets. Well, honey, I was getting ready to do a number on that bus driver, but my mother wasn't for it — you know, she's kinda quiet and didn't want to be embarrassed — and so I just got all mad inside.

Me: So there are times when we want to be assertive — we want to let go and tell it like it is, but we don't — we hold back for a variety of reasons.

Group: Yeah — that's it.

Me: Then maybe what we should do is look at some of the things that hold us back and some of the ways we can let go.

Byron: (Quiet up to this time) That's what I'm here to check out.

Me: In order to find out how each one of us may hold back in some ways and not in others — I'd like to pass out what I call an Assertive Inventory. (I start passing out the Assertive Inventory — see Chapter VI.) It's just twenty different kinds of questions that you can check off answers to.

John: Who's going to see it — I mean, after it's filled out?

Me: Good point — I should have mentioned that everything that takes place here is strictly confidential — I talk with nobody about what goes on and I would like to be sure that everyone feels the same way (There are general nods of agreement). As far as the inventory, John, there's nothing real world shaking in it. It just gives us an idea of what type of problems to start dealing with in talking about assertive training. There's no score or nothing. Just answer as openly and honestly as possible.

Bertha: Just be assertive with the question?

Me: Right on, Bertha.

(The group finishes the Assertive Inventory)

John: Do you want our names on it?

Bertha: Of course the man wants your name on it — how's he gonna know it's you?

John: I wasn't talkin to you.

Bertha: Well, I'm talking to you.

Me: (smiling) Yes — your name on the sheet would be very helpful.

(All the Assertive Inventory sheets are turned in)

Me: Alright. There's something else that would be helpful to getting us to understand ourselves better and figure out why we hold back and keep from really expressing ourselves sometimes.

Step II

Me: I would like for everyone to take a sheet of paper and a pencil. Draw three lines down the sheet of paper so that you can make four equal columns. (I take my sheet and demonstrate). I am going to give you a word or heading for each column. At the top of the first column (the one on the left side) put the word "somebody." Your paper should look like this:

Somebody			

Now under "Somebody" let's try to think of the people in the past that we wish we had been honest, direct and to the point with — somebody to whom we wish we had really said what we felt. Even if we don't have a name for the person, put down a description, like "the busdriver that gave my mother a hard time." It could even be a person that you still have to deal with currently or in the future. Really any "somebody" that you can think of. To help you, I'm going to describe seven different kinds of situations in which we usually have to deal with people — just to get you to thinking and remembering. OK? Any questions?

Byron: What if I can't think of a somebody?

Me: That means you either never held back from expressing your feelings to a person, or if you did hold back you can't remember.

Byron: So what do I do?

Me: Just relax and as I mention the various situations in which we deal with people see if you can recall a time when you kind of held back.

Byron: (Nodding his head) That's cool. I can dig it.

Me: O.K. Let's relax and think of the different "somebodys" that we wish we had kinda straightened out or got off our backs in the past — or present — or future. (Long pauses and I begin to quietly describe situations from the Survival Ladder.) In our daily routine activities — waiters, bank clerks, busdrivers, salesclerks, telephone operators, train, plane, bus clerks or people you come in contact with. Secretaries, bartenders, police — you beginning to get the idea? (Group begins to write and a few help me out by mentioning roles that I haven't mentioned.) O.K., just briefly name or describe the person so you will remember who it is when you come back to them. (Pause) Category 2 is leisure and recreation — people you would party with, acquaintances, peers, friends. Somebody who hit on your old lady (or old man) and you should have come on strong with or somebody who might have tried to put you down in a social situation. (Pause) Next is the home category — parents, husbands, in-laws, brothers, sisters and you name it. Let's not take up the whole page now (laughter) just choose a few. (Pause) The fourth category is community — neighbors, church committees and things like that — any "somebody" that you might have had to deal with — don't worry if you think of some of the same people in other categories — this is just to stimulate your thinking. (Pause) Category #5 is school or education for any of you who need to remember teachers, administrators and schoolmates. (Pause) The job category is #6 — here we have supervisors, bosses, people over us or people under us as well as people we work with. Take your time — there is no hurry — if you want more paper; we have it. Just think about the different people that you have had to deal with and the times that you wish you had said what was on your mind — either afraid, too cautious or didn't feel that it was the right time or place. O.K. (Pause) Category #7 the last situation is institutional — that means where some of us have had to deal with social workers, police, probation officers, correctional officers — maybe secretaries again or maybe wards or patients depending on how we have been involved with institutions — you know like some of us have had to deal with welfare people and maybe some of us have been on the other side and worked for some institutions or agencies. Just think of the "somebody" you wish you had dealt with and got it clear where you were coming from. I see some people still writing. There sure must be a lot of people we want to straighten out. I should name this the "I wish I had of" list. (Pause) O.K., let's finish up.

Now, let's go back and put titles or names at the top of the other three columns. Let's put Age for column 2, Sex for column 3 and Race for column #4. Now go down your description of each somebody and after each one say whether they are young, middle-aged or old — male or female and what race they are. If you don't know, guess — yes, even the sex.

Mary: What's old — I don't know what you want when you say old, middle age or young?

Me: Well, let's just put it down the way you see it — we can get to specifics later — for now it will just be the way you see it.

Byron: Does that mean I can put down an oreo as white? (laughter from the group follows)

Alex: Yeah, I know some Toms too that don't even know what they are themselves!

Me: O.K. (smile) Let's be liberal and if its a member call them a member.

Byron: We'll have some honorary spooks then (puts his hand out to get five from Alex. Everyone cracks up with laughter).

Me: (After a pause to allow everyone to complete filling in the columns.) All right — we've got the different somebodys put down and somewhat described. Byron, I even saw you writing.

Byron: Yeah, man, I forgot how many enemies I had till I got started.

Step III

Me: All right — there's one more thing I would like for the group to do while we are filling things out — it's a brief questionnaire with only six questions (the questionnaire on black and white language which appears in Chapter VI).

Alex: What are they?

Me: Here they are — just pass them around and follow the written instructions. Let's not cheat or copy from someone else (laughter). O.K. — you don't have to study it — just put down your honest response — and total each section, we'll discuss it later. Again, I would like for you to put your name on the sheet unless you have serious objections. (Depending on the group, I may read the instructions myself to save any embarrassment about reading.)

O.K., everyone finished the questionnaire? Please total each section and pass it back to me. Also place your name on the "somebody" sheet and pass it to me. (As the sheets are handed to me I briefly scan them, noting some scores and the contents of columns 2, 3 and 4 of the "somebody" list.) After shuffling through the papers I usually notice the descriptions cover the gamut of different ages, sex and races.

Step IV:

Me: Earlier when we were talking about past situations and reasons why we didn't speak up we found that people mentioned different things — like not knowing how somebody was going to take it or wanting to stay on someone's good side. From your papers I can see we have problems with people of different ages, sex and races. Because we function in a skin-color-conscious society and because traditionally skin color has been more important than age or sex in this society, I would like to have us start off having a dual focus — looking at two things at the same time or at least keeping two things in mind. Let's start off by discussing the idea of expressing ourselves in general — what I'll call being assertive and at the same time consider the implications of the black (or white) experience as it affects such expression. I mean the difference in being assertive with someone white and being assertive with someone black.

Byron: There's really no difference, champ, I say what I got to say to anybody.

Me: That may be true for you, Byron, but let's hold off and we'll check that idea out. You know. Is that cool?

Byron: Yeah, rap on.

(I usually like to end the session at this point and tell everyone we will begin the next meeting with some background about assertiveness and the black experience.)

Session 2

Completion Step IV:

Me: As you remember I mentioned that we would take a dual approach or a dual focus — keeping two things in mind, being assertive and the black experience.

Group: (Nodding) Yeah, that's right.

Alex: Question. When you say black do you mean skin color or in one's mind because there are a lot of "white" black folks, you dig, and they may have the skin color but their minds are fucked up.

Me: Good point, Alex, but for now let's consider them exceptions and deal with what we would generally consider as people who are black by skin color and know that that is what they are. Later we can get into passing and social class and being bourgeois.

Byron: Yeah, like check it out, Hare talks about those Toms that live in Never-Negro-Land. (Group laughter and palm slapping at this reference to the book the *Black Anglo-Saxons* by Nathan Hare, a figure known to many students from the Black Community.)

Me: Yeah, that's cool, but for now let's deal with what we might call the average black person.

Group: (Good naturedly nods approval)

Me: O.K. So there's two things we're talking about — being assertive and how that may be affected by being black (or white). First let me say what I mean by being assertive — I mean honestly expressing yourself without intending to harm anyone or put them down. (Some hands go up and there may be a few who attempt to ask questions.) Wait a minute — hold your questions please — let me first outline some general ideas and then we can get into the questions. If you think you may forget, then write your question down.

Alright — so by assertion I will mean honestly expressing yourself without the intention of it being harmful or a put down. When we intend to harm someone — not just physically — I mean verbally, or when we intend to insult them or put them down — that would be aggressive or be called aggressive. If we want to respond to something or want to express ourselves but we go along with the program and smile or just don't do nothing or act like everything's all right — that type of behavior is called passive.

Now the way that we have been raised and the things that we have learned have a lot to do with how we act. And it has a lot to do with how free we are when we get older or when we are no longer children. The way that we have been told to *feel* things can sometimes eliminate our choices of whether to be assertive instead of aggressive or passive. I see by the expressions on your faces that I may be losing some of you so let me back up, O.K.? What I'm talking about is three basic ways of dealing with people — shinin them on and not letting them know what you think, I call that passive; coming on strong, insulting people and making them feel bad *on purpose*, I call that aggressive and then — well, let me put it this way — those are the main two ways we tend to act based upon the way most of us have been raised. Remember last week when I asked if there were times that we held back and didn't express ourselves directly and just about everybody agreed? Remember when we agreed that, for whatever reasons we wanted to give, there were times we really didn't say what was on our minds? O.K. I admit that it may be cool at times to hold back — like to keep yourself from being fired — but I'm now talking about all those times when we really had no major *survival* reasons for laying dead — we just plain didn't express our honest feelings and most of the time ended up feeling bad because we didn't say what we should have said (nodding agreement from the group). Good — O.K., now you got the feeling — it's like we either come on strong like we're going to do somebody in or we just lay dead and play it cool. I'm saying that we act that way because of past experiences and the way we have been taught — in fact, let me give you the technical name for what I'm talking about — it's called the socialization process — (drop that on somebody and it will blow their minds) — but that is really the correct word for what I'm talking about and that's the way the sociological and psychological books will sometimes refer to it. And all it really means is that a person being dependent on others for a long period of time starts to take on the ideas, beliefs, values and attitudes of the people, the culture and the society immediately around him. It's just like language — we are biologically able to speak any language — I mean when we are born we could really learn any language — Chinese, German, Greek — but we learned English because it was part of our immediate environment and was given to us by our primary group — that means parents and family. You see, it's like when we are born we are turned over to the family to get us ready to participate in society. We are socialized or given the so-called "right way to do things" as defined by the particular society — it could mean eat with your fingers, eat with chopsticks or eat with knife and fork — it's whatever that particular society or group of people defines as "appropriate." A famous social psychologist used a term I like; his name was W.I. Thomas and he talked about "Definition of the situation." Well, this is what we are basically taught — the ideas about etiquette, about being on time, about patriotism or about God — all of this is society's definition of the situation. The socializing agents are the things outside the immediate family that helped put those beliefs and values into us — the school, the church, our peers or friends and the mass media — all of these things get us to see ourselves a certain way — give us a self concept, you've heard that word before. So very early we are taught to share our toys with brothers, sisters or friends — not to hurt Uncle Frank's feelings if he was cheap and didn't give us anything for Christmas or to be careful not to say things that would hurt people's feelings. We were taught to act "nice" and do things and say things so that people would like us. (Lots of head nodding and agreeing comments from the group.)

John: Yeah, I just gotta say this, Dr. Cheek: I was raised in the South you know and I was taught to say yes sir and no sir to any adult and man — you bet not get caught being disrespectful or talkin out of turn — it was speak when you were spoken to and be seen and not heard or those old "Sunday go to meetin" folks would straighten you out — so I know where you comin from.

Me: Thanks, John, that's the kinda thing I mean — we were conditioned very early to act in a certain way towards people — usually in a way that would not stamp us as being selfish or as disregarding the feelings of others — like the virtues were to be kind, polite, considerate and (someone from the group says "Like a boy scout") well, yes, that's as good a description as any — like a boy scout — a white boy scout. For you see these were ideas that basically reflected the white, middle class way of doing things.

Now, one way parents and society control our behavior is by making us feel guilty or anxious if we do something they think is wrong. So as we grow up and want to play with all of our toys without sharing, we are made to feel guilty — or if we take somebody's cake at the table we are made to feel bad and feel guilty. It's not that our parents or people raising us don't love us — it's that they are afraid we might get out of control — too aggressive, and it is also the way they have been taught — we just pass our child training down from one generation to the next. So you see, we usually end up with two forms of behavior — either taking, taking, taking from other people — laying dead, being cool and not expressing our honest feelings directly; or we end up super pissed off and explode with the intention of hurting someone's feelings or some other part of their body — that's aggressive. The in-between behavior that is usually not taught us is what is called being assertive — not intending to hurt anyone's feelings but being straightforward and leveling with a person even if they may not like it.

Mary: Well, doesn't that mean that you don't care how the other person feels?

Me: No, Mary, it means that you are more concerned with being honest and open and letting that person know how *you* feel — I guess it's a matter of priority.

Mary: Well, that sounds pretty selfish!

Me: Yeah, maybe it does. Which again tells us the way we have been taught in this society — to be concerned with self is bad. I'm not sure that's always true. Maybe we should give the other person a little more credit for being able to handle a straightforward and honest expression from us.

Bertha: That's right, why should I always be the one gettin mad and holding it in all the time — shit let them get mad too — spread it around.

Me: (smiling) Well, Bertha. I see what you mean but I think I'm talking about expressing yourself way before you get to the point of being mad — like a steam valve — you know — lettin a little bit out instead of letting the pressure all build up and then exploding.

Bertha: Um-huh (not sounding too convinced).

Me: Well, we'll talk more about that later — let me finish up this idea about the socialization process and how it tends to keep us from being assertive. I haven't talked about the part that relates to the black experience. The average white person has been taught how to be a good boy scout — or how to feel guilty or anxious if they are aggressive at the wrong times — I mean sometimes its' O.K. to be aggressive like in business or in athletics since our society stresses competition — getting what you want at another person's expense — but on most other occasions and socially speaking we are expected to be considerate of others. In other words we are supposed to feel guilty or anxious if we violate the rules of the game — and most of us learn pretty early when we can be aggressive and when we are expected to get along.

Step V:

Well, for black people in this society the rules historically have been a little different — in case you haven't heard (the group snickers). Traditionally speaking, black folks have been forced to be passive toward whites for purposes of survival. Is there anyone in here who hasn't heard of the game of black survival — the game with the rule that you tell the white man what he wants to hear?

Byron: Yeah, but all that shit has changed, brother.

John: (Directing his comments to Byron) When that white policeman stopped your ass the other night, I didn't hear you being too aggressive — you sounded just like one of those shufflin niggers to me (laughter from the group).

Byron: That ain't got nothin to do with it, man, that's the police — that's a whole different thing.

Me: No, not necessarily. You see even with the police, one can be assertive — in a way that's how Huey Newton started off in Oakland — knowing his rights, not being insulting and just being honest and straightforward. Of course, we all know, the situation and the people got carried away, but the principle of being assertive was there at first.

But, the point I am making is that, originally most blacks were socialized in the south, under Jim Crow laws that have resulted in what I call the "Jim Crow Halo Effect." That means that whether we are conscious of it or not, some attitudes and values from those days of white oppression have been handed down and affect the behavior of blacks today. Two immediate examples are language and inter- or intraracial attitudes. I'm talking about black-white and black-black interaction. With blacks being separated from whites through Jim Crowism there was the opportunity for blacks to develop their own language — or I should correctly say their own verbal and non-verbal means of communicating. Also, particular attitudes developed with regard to the ways that blacks related to whites in contrast to the ways they related to each other. I refer to this whole thing as connected to the psycho-historical background of the black experience. For a long period of time blacks could not vote, blacks could not use white bathrooms, could not sit in the same section at the movies, could not swim in the same pool or be buried in the same cemetery. Blacks for awhile in this country were in separate armies, could not play football, baseball or basketball either together with/or against whites. They were separate but equal under the law — the Supreme Court decided that in 1896 Plessy vs. Ferguson.

Alma: I read about that in history, but the teacher didn't say all of that about Jim Crow.

Me: Well, Alma, I'm only mentioning this as it relates to the need for us to be aware of how black families have taught their children certain ways to survive — and some of those ways and ideas may still be with us and in the black community. There was a time when you dared not think about talking back to a white person. If you were in a line and a white came up, it was understood they were to be served first.

Byron: Man, that makes me mad.

John: Me, too.

Me: It's no sense in getting mad. I'm bringing it up because it's possible for you to let other people do this to you — people who are not white can also do you in — and it's being done every day. Today, it's usually not the white man who encourages you to party instead of studying — it's not the white man that keeps us from speaking up to each other — in our marriages, in our families, to our friends. So, historically and maybe even today, whites may be part of the problem, but let's be careful and look at ourselves too. Since I feel this is a very important area for us to get into and to be real clear about, I'm going to ask you to fill out another short questionnaire.

Alex: What is this one about?

Me: I call it the GAP questionnaire (see Chapter VI). That stands for Group Awareness Profile. It just gives some indication of how we perceive blacks and whites and how we think they perceive us.

Byron: I don't need no questionnaire to know what's happenin with rabbits (black in-group reference to whites).

Me: I can understand that Byron, but this just gives me an objective picture from each person that is useful for me to do a better job with the group.

Byron: That's cool, that's cool (said in a kind of condescending manner).

Me: O.K. It's a questionnaire with just 12 questions — let's fill it out like the others — just straightforward, honest and direct. (The questionnaire is handed out, worked on and collected.)

Session 3

Alex: So how does all that stuff we talked about fit in with assertive training?

Me: Good point, Alex. What I've been doing up to now has been just to kinda lay the foundation for some other things we're going to do. Right now I'm going to ask you to listen to something and answer some questions about it. (At this point I pass out a single sheet of paper to each person that has seven questions on it.) What I want you to do is just to listen for a few minutes and then briefly answer each question. (Here I play either a record or tape of very rhythmic tambourine-shaking, soulful gospel music — I usually choose "Swing Down Sweet Chariot" by Bessie Griffin and the Gospel Pearls. After the music is on for awhile I usually, for emphasis, slowly repeat the questions written on the paper.) Just answer each question as completely as possible —

1) Do you feel anything, yes or no?
2) How does the music make you feel?
3) What does it make you want to express — if anything?
4) What does it make you want to do — if anything?
5) Did you do it?
6) Would you do it?
7) What does it make you think about or remember — if anything?

(I then collect the papers and turn the music off).

John: Hey — don't turn that off (The group supports his good natured protest).

Me: Uh-huh, that woke you up, didn't it!

John: (along with the others) Sho nuff did.

Me: Can anyone tell me what just happened — I mean just a few minutes ago?

Bertha: You played some down home music — that we got to feeling and then you came in with some questions.

Me: What else did anyone observe?

Mary: Some foot pattin.

Alma: Some hip moving (group laughs).

Byron: Some soul rockin and finger poppin.

John: Right on.

Me: That's it — that's it right there — the desire, and for some of you the actual behavior of expressing honest, direct, open feelings without the thought of putting anyone down. Most of you were not shy about tapping your feet, moving your heads and in other ways expressing yourself — nonverbally. Given a little more time we could have gotten to shoutin and feeling the spirit.

Alma: That's the truth.

Me: The reason I use this as an example is because it shows us the real ingredients of being assertive. Being confident about how you feel — not being worried over what others think about what we are doing — not being self conscious or worried about hurting someone's feelings — the music just gave us a natural feeling of doing your own thing — not being hung up, inhibited and up tight — am I right?

Group: Yeah-yeah, that's about it.

Me: I don't want to get to preachin, but I just want you to grab hold of that feeling — that feeling of being spontaneous, of being yourself, of just letting what you feel be expressed. Just like at the Earth, Wind and Fire concert at the Hollywood Bowl. This woman jumped up and got to shaking her hips — the man sitting in back of her said, "Would you please stop waving that thing around before you hit somebody?"

Group: (Laughs and slaps palms).

Me: The point is that when we are really assertive, we don't get hung up on those problems that were talked about in the first session — you remember those things about hurting someone's feelings, staying on somebody's good side or not trusting yourself as to how it's going to come out? That doesn't mean there isn't a skill in learning how to talk to people — but it means that we let it flow and come out kinda spontaneously — like groovin to the music — you dig?

Byron: That sounds pretty hip — I mean, that's pretty together.

Me: All right, let's really get into it next session.

Session 4

Step VII:

Me: O.K., let's get right into the basic elements of assertiveness. You remember we talked about "somebody" and we described the person on paper.

Group: Right.

Me: Well, we can call that somebody the target person. Then there is you, the communicator or person who expresses themselves. Then there is also what is being expressed — or what I refer to as the message. (I usually draw these three symbols on a chalk board in any way that resembles two people and something in between them.) When we get to our practice exercises, it's going to be necessary to know about you and the target person in order to evaluate the message.

Mary: Does that go back to that black language, white language thing you had us fill out?

Me: Yes, Mary, you see that little questionnaire alerted me and you to the different ways a black person could express themselves.

Byron: And there's a whole lot of ways that you can't get on that paper.

Me: Correct, Byron. You really beat me to my next point. In order to help us evaluate whether or not the message is assertive we should pay attention to at least seven things — 1) eye contact, 2) body posture, 3) hand movements, 4) facial expression, 5) voice, 6) the content of the message and 7) when we choose to deliver the message.

Alex: All them things can make a difference depending on where you come from — I mean it depends on your background or culture how you interpret all of that.

Me: Right. What did you have in mind Alex?

Alex: Well, I'm from the West Indies, Trinidad, and sometimes I get very excited and talk fast and loud and some whites think that I'm angry.

Byron: Some niggers think so too. You can sure screw up the English language.

Alex: Man, I speak better than you — all you know how to do is cuss.

Step VIII:

Me: O.K., let's cool it — you dudes sure got assertive quick. Getting back to you, Alex — your point is well taken. Depending on your background you read different things into something like people's voice, its tone, inflection and volume. All right, let's practice a little so that we can get these ideas straight. How about taking one of those "somebodys" that you wrote about in our first session?

Group: (Mumbling, looking at each other with no volunteers).

Me: All right, then let's use the example you gave us, Bertha, the bus driver that wouldn't take your transfer tickets. Let's all get quiet and each of us imagine the situation of a bus driver refusing our transfer tickets. This time we respond in an assertive manner.

Mary: Do I have to close my eyes?

Me: Do anything that helps you to imagine the situation and what you would do.

Group: (Quiet, some with eyes closed and some staring into space.)

Me: Who's first?

John: Let Byron go first.

Me: Byron — are you ready?

Byron: You want to hear what I would say?

Me: (I nod approval.)

Byron: Looka here, mothafucka, you either take this ticket or I'll jam it up your ass.

Group: (Muffling laughter and looking at me.)

Me: O.K. Byron, would you call that assertive, aggressive or passive?

Byron: Definitely aggressive.

Me: Why?

Byron: Because I intended to hurt the dude's feelings — and his body.

Me: And describe the target person as to race.

Byron: White on white.

Me: Do you think you would get cooperation from the bus driver?

Byron: Maybe — depends on how much heart the dude has.

Me: Let me put it this way — obviously you imagined a situation in which the bus driver was low on your survival ladder — in other words you really didn't care about riding the bus. Now a lot of times when we don't care we can easily be either passive or aggressive. In fact most blacks, because of the psycho-historical things that I talked about, have usually stressed either the passive or aggressive modes. I would like for all of you to focus on being assertive — put away the intention of putting someone down for awhile and also put away the passive approach. Let us all try to focus on dealing with each other — and I mean black people dealing with black people — and dealing with others — I mean blacks dealing with whites — in a manner that is open, honest, direct and not downing the person. In a way I think we have too much of that kind of crap. And I'm especially sad to see blacks treating each other in unkind and hostile ways. All right, let's see if someone else is ready.

Alma: I would do it differently. I would just tell the man that he had to take the transfer ticket because that's the only way I could get home.

Me: Let me be the bus driver and you get on my bus, Alma.

Alma: O.K., say something.

Me: Well, all right, imagine that you and your mother get on my bus and hand me the transfers. I say, "Look, lady, these transfers are no good — you have to pay a full fare."

Alma: I'm sorry, the other driver gave them to me.

Me: (as bus driver) Look, lady, either pay the fare or get off the bus.

Alma: I can't get off. This is the only way me and my mother can get home. Please take the ticket?

Me: (as bus driver) No, I'm sorry lady. The rules don't allow for me to accept those transfers.

Alma: Won't you please give us a break this time?

Me: (as bus driver) I'm sorry you will have to get off the bus — or pay.

Alma: (Looking confused at this point and not saying anything.)

Me: What's wrong, Alma?

Alma: What do I say now — do I pay or get off the bus?

Me: Oh-oh-oh — you goofed. Stay on the darn bus — don't pay nothin.

Alma: (Looking hurt) Well, you get up here and do it.

Me: How would you label your response, Alma?

Alma: I was assertive — at first, but then I started to get — well when you wouldn't agree, I guess I got sorta passive.

Me: You started pleading, didn't you?

Alma: (Quietly) Yes.

Me: That's all right for the first day. You see, the components of assertiveness come in really handy when you think about them. What was your intent, Alma?

Alma: To be assertive.

Me: Group — what was lacking in Alma's attempt to communicate an assertive message?

Group: (Various members) Her voice gave way. Her eyes looked down. She didn't sound sure of herself.

Me: You see, Alma — all those things put together don't present an assertive image.

Alma: I see.

Me: That's why I refused to take the ticket — in a way you encouraged me *not* to give in because your assertiveness came apart. Do you understand what I mean?

Alma: Yes.

Me: Remember the reaction to the gospel music — spontaneous, lots of energy, enthusiasm, force, projection, confidence — you get the picture?

Alma: (smiling) Yeah — I hear that.

Me: Let me be the passenger and I get on the bus. Who will be the bus driver?

Alex: I will.

Me: (Handing Alex the ticket.)

Alex: I'm sorry, mister, the transfer's no good.

Me: The last driver gave them to us as transfer tickets.

Alex: But they are no good — you have to pay or get off my bus.

Me: That's up to you, I'm not paying and I'm not getting off the bus.

Alex: But you have to.

Me: No, I don't — I'm giving you the transfer tickets that the last bus driver gave me. If there is a mistake, it's the company's mistake not mine.

Alex: I'll just call the cops.

Me: Then I will report you to the bus company as not being cooperative or courteous to a customer — you will lose your job.

Alex: Hey, man, you not suppose to say that.

(The group starts laughing and Alex shakes his head.)

Alex: That's pretty good, that's pretty good.

Me: (Turning to the group) Was I serious?

Byron: To the bone, baby, to the bone — the bus driver couldn't deal with that.

Me: What I tried to model for you was how to look, feel, talk, act and project seriousness in your assertive message. Stick to the basic language — don't talk too much — don't argue. Say what you mean and mean what you say.

(For the remainder of the session I have the group break into threes — two practicing being either the passenger or the bus driver and the third person acting as a critical observer. The observers are told to pay close attention and see how well the words and actions fit the assertive model. Following each practice role play, the observer offers feedback on the components of assertiveness to the others.)

Session 5

Information from the Assertive Inventory and GAP questionnaire are used for this session and those that follow. Individual attention is given to those Assertive Inventory questions that have a "yes" answer. This inventory is used in conjunction with the GAP questionnaire so that the facilitator can be sensitive to the problems the client may have expressing him or herself to a black or white person.

TEACHING BLACK ASSERTION

In summary, the following format is use for assertive behavior training with black clients:

1 to 5 — The five preparation steps are provided prior to the action phase.

6 — The assertiveness — music connection is demonstrated and/or discussed.

7 — The basic elements of assertion are reviewed (eye contact, body posture, hand movements, facial expression, voice, message content and timing). The problems regarding the intent of the

message as related to different target persons is demonstrated and discussed.

8 — Practice sessions are conducted based on immediate problems of the client or information from the GAP or Assertive Inventory. Modeling of assertiveness takes place.

9 — Actual trials of assertive behavior take place in "real life."

10 — After assertive trials are discussed, additional real life situations are attempted and discussed with the facilitator and group.

Frequently, the practitioner is called upon to put parts of the suggested procedure into immediate operation, based on the client's needs. This means that, depending upon the presenting problem, there is not sufficient time to go through the various steps — one or two of them must be quickly selected and put into action. From past experience, many black clients need assistance in developing the type of message that conventionally oriented whites will perceive as assertive (not putting them down) instead of aggressive (putting them down). This is an especially tricky problem for the following reasons:

1) Whites are looking and listening for aggressiveness in blacks,

2) Blacks are hesitant to patronize whites or alter their black style of communication,

3) The power relationship still exists with whites being in positions of control over most blacks.

The didactic approach seems to offer the clearest solution. Let the black client know how the target person will possibly perceive the message, despite the intent, and allow the client the choice of which communication style is to be used. The approach concentrates on steps 7 and 8 of the above format. An example of this is as follows:

Situation: A black patient has lost his hall card in a maximum security hospital. He goes to the supervisory nurse to obtain a reason for the disciplinary action. He also plans to find out how his privileges can be restored. He complains to me that the nurse refused to listen to him.

Me: You say that the nurse just plain wouldn't cooperate with you, is that right?

Patient: That's what I said.

Me: Tell me exactly what you said to her.

Patient: It's a man.

Me: All right, tell me what you said to him.

Patient: I told him I wanted to know why they took my hall card away.

Me: Look — make believe I'm the nurse and you walk up to me and talk to me exactly like you talked to him. I want you to do everything exactly the same, all right? Don't leave out nothing — O.K.?

Patient: Yeah.

Me: O.K., walk up to me and begin.

Patient: (Walks up to me with an angry frown on his face.) Looka here, man, I wanna know why you all always fuckin with me — what did I do now that made you all take my goddamn hall card away? (The patient said this while vigorously shaking his finger in my face.)

Me: (Just quietly look at the patient without saying a word.)

Patient: Well, what's wrong?

Me: Man, was the nurse white?

Patient: Yeah.

Me: Do you really think he's used to black people talking to him that way?

Patient: (Quietly stares at me.)

Me: I mean even if it was a brother I would wonder if he wanted to hear all of that, but at least he would have been used to it.

Patient: I wasn't trying to hurt his feelings or nothin. I was just upset about them messin with my hall card.

Me: If you really wanted to be aggressive and put him down what would you have said?

Patient: (After quietly staring at the floor.) I guess I would have said near the same thing.

Me: Look, when you get upset you may not intend to hurt someone's feelings but the way it comes out it does. Of course the other way of dealing with the problem would have been not to say anything at all — just shine the dude on — that would have been passive. From listening to you, you just seem to come on too strong.

Patient: That's right — I tell it like it is.

Me: Can I suggest a better way of asserting yourself with the nurse?

Patient: Yeah, lemme hear.

Me: When you walk up to him it wouldn't hurt to say "excuse me" in case you are interrupting him or something.

Patient: He wasn't doing nothing important.

Me: Look, man, you don't know that. I'm going to tell you how to talk to white folks — now you want to listen, or you want to argue?

Patient: I'm listening.

Me: All right. So first show some courtesy. Most people like courtesy — I'm sure even you do — don't you?

Patient: (Smiling and nods agreement.)

Me: So say something like, "excuse me" or "I beg your pardon, can I talk to you for a minute" or if you want to be fancy you can say "Can I have a word with you" — you dig?

Patient: Talk that shit?

Me: I'm serious, brother. You just can't come on strong and think people — black or white, but especially white — are going to listen to you. So get your act together. You don't have to Tom, you can be yourself — but, you know, you got to put it the right way.

Patient: Yeah, I'm checkin it out.

Me: So, you start the conversation in a courteous way — "Excuse me" (Wait for him to turn your way or give you his attention.) "I'd like to find out why my hall card was taken. I would appreciate it if you would talk to me about it." Can you try that? Notice, I didn't wave my finger in the dude's face either.

Patient: Seems simple enough.

(Patient and I role play the scene until he feels comfortable with this new approach.)

The feedback offered in this example provides the patient with needed information as to how he appears to others — especially to those who are white. With this new awareness the patient is helped to evaluate his message and choose a more effective approach.

CHAPTER IX

Lifting the Veil of Color

"I began to marvel at how smoothly
the black boys acted out the roles that
the white race had mapped out for
them. Most of them were not
conscious of living a special, separate,
stunted way of life."
Richart Wright
Black Boy

Hopefully, the message is clear. Assertive behavior when expressed by blacks has a different impact and requires a different approach and understanding. The black athletes of the 400-meter relay team who mounted the first place podium at the 1968 Olympics decided to honestly and openly express themselves. They raised their black fists above their heads in what became known as the black power salute. No words — only a non-verbal token of their pride in being black in addition to being American. They were blasted for misuse of the Olympics. They were condemned for "inappropriate" behavior — according to white standards. The black community understood and supported this act of assertive behavior — the black community was aware of the intent and understood the message. It was indeed a message that non-verbally stated that black people are here and cannot be ignored or called part of the melting pot — we didn't melt. Blacks were not at the Olympics just as *Americans*, but as *black Americans*. If black Americans are deluded by events like the Olympics, then it is possible that they will look at America and think that South Boston doesn't exist — that affirmative action is not necessary — that racial discrimination in schools, housing and employment is a myth. But those black athletes remembered that the word "Nigger" is very much part of the white American's heritage and tradition. And so the conflict over appropriate assertive behavior went on. In the 1972 Olympics the black 400-meter champion, Vince Matthews, was banned from Olympic competition for life for improper behavior during the playing of the American national anthem. He was exchanging comments with his black teammate, Wayne Collett, which was "perceived" as being disrespectful. A white American Olympian however could wear a cap during the same type ceremony and be free of having any disrespect attributed to his behavior.

These conflicts in attitudes, perceptions and values are part of the American cultural fabric within which the issue of blacks and whites must be addressed. These conflicts are frequently brought into the counseling or therapeutic relationship. Whites know it and blacks feel it. White practitioners know they are ill-prepared by either multi-cultural education or by training from a black perspective to deal with black clients and black standards. Most black clients can feel the ambivalence and awkwardness. At times, even the black practitioner is sucked up into the white academic pressure cooker and comes out acting more like a white colleague than his or her black self. There are extremely few black role models involved in the training process who can help counter white standards for the black student drowning in Western European, white male dominated social dogma. This book struggles against that imbalance.

If white therapists are going to become more effective with black clients they need to counter their white indoctrination with training and exposure from a black perspective. If black therapists are going to guide black clients into more healthy, fulfilling and dignified lives, they need to continue the development and modification of approaches like assertive training — from a black perspective.

Reflecting upon the issue of white therapists treating black clients, my colleague, Dr. Robert Alberti, brought to my attention the issue of ethics. As I began to consider the implications of professional standards and ethics, relevant questions gradually seemed to form. Should you offer to treat a client if your background and training has not prepared you to deal with his/her perceptions of reality?

What does it mean, if a white therapist knows little or nothing about black lifestyles, black patterns of communication, or the significance to blacks of skin color, ethnic identity, or regional differences? Should the competence of such a practitioner with regard to treating blacks be an issue? Should such "cultural unawareness" pose a question of ethics for such professional organizations as those of psychiatrists, psychologists, social workers, teachers and ministers? Of course these questions touch on the assumption of skill and ability being assured through academic degrees or credentials. But we have already seen that most of the training is offered by whites with hardly any regard for the value or need of a multi-cultural perspective. What those degrees and credentials actually mean is that the recipient has learned from anglo institutions those techniques and skills "appropriate" for dealing with white clients. What about native American clients? Chinese or Japanese clients? Latino clients?

In most situations, the client must depend on the integrity of honesty of the therapists in admitting that they have limits in understanding ethnic minorities who function with different cultural standards. Obviously there must be increasing awareness among professional associations and training programs that education is needed which will increase multi-racial understanding.

We need more attention to multi-cultural and cross-cultural research in the institutions that train our therapists and practitioners. We need more information as to how definitions of assertive, aggressive and passive behavior may change by virtue of social class, region and/or culture as well as other overlooked variables. We need a deeper understanding of the black woman's assertive and aggressive styles as contrasted with those of the white female. More time, energy and resources need to be invested in developing college and graduate school courses that deal with racial and cultural differences. These courses should be initially team taught by competent black and white instructors. In addition, they should be required courses and not elective. Not until then will we begin to have black and white therapists who possess the exposure to a multi-cultural body of knowledge that will hopefully lead to being more sensitive, knowledgeable and racially aware leaders in the field of mental health.

The racial problems that have and will continue to plague the helping professions are not insurmountable. They are part of the American society that has for too long attempted to ignore the great schism that exists because of the realities of skin color. This reality was eloquently discussed by one of America's most gifted black intellectuals, W.E.B. DuBois, during his 60th year when he wrote (1968):

> And then — the Veil, the Veil of color. It drops as drops the night on southern seas — vast, sudden, unanswering. There is Hate behind it, and Cruelty and Tears. As one peers through its

intricate, unfathomable pattern of ancient, old, old design, one sees blood and guilt and misunderstanding. And yet it hangs there, this Veil between then and now, between Pale and Colored and Black and White — between you and me. Surely it is but a thought — thing, tenuous, intangible; yet just as surely is it true and terrible and not in our little day may you and I lift it. We may feverishly unravel its edges and even climb slow with giant shears to where its ringed and gilded top nestles close to the throne of Eternity. But as we work and climb we shall see through streaming eyes and hear with aching ears, lynching and murder, cheating and despising, degrading and lying, so flashed and flashed through this vast hanging darkness that the Doer never sees the Deed and the Victim knows not the Victor and Each hate all in wild and bitter ignorance.[23]

Let us take heed and deal assertively with the task of lifting this veil.

FOOTNOTE:

[23] DuBois, W.E.B., *The Autobiography of W.E.B. DuBois*, N.Y.: International Publishers, ©1968. Used by permission.

ASSERTIVE BLACK ... PUZZLED WHITE

BIBLIOGRAPHY

Alberti, R.E., and Emmons, M.L., *Stand Up, Speak Out, Talk Back*. New York: Pocket Books (Simon and Schuster), 1975.

Alberti, R.E., and Emmons, M.L., *Your Perfect Right*. San Luis Obispo, California: Impact Publishers, Inc., 1974.

Andrews, M., and Owens, P.T., *Black Language*. Los Angeles: Seymour-Smith, Publisher (P.O. Box 25228, Los Angeles, CA 90025), 1973.

Ash, P., Awkard, J., Hicks, L.H., Hoffman, M., and Porter, J., The negro psychologist in America. In Wilcox, R.C. (Ed.), *Psychological Consequences of Being a Black American*. New York: John Wiley and Sons, 1971.

Baldwin, J., *Notes of a Native Son*. New York: Bantam Books, 1964.

Bankiotes, P.G., Bankiotes, F.G., and Schumacher, L.C., Language compatibility and minority group counseling. *Journal of Counseling Psychology*, 1972, *19*, 255-256.

Banks, G., and Carkhuff, R., Training as a preferred mode of facilitating relations between races and generations. *Journal of Counseling Psychology*, 1970, *17*, 413-418.

Barnes, E.J., Counseling and the black student: The need for a new view. In Jones, R.L. (Ed.), *Black Psychology*. New York: Harper and Row, 1972.

Baughman, E.E., *Black Americans*. New York: Academic Press, 1971.

Billingsley, A., *Black Families in White America*. Englewood Cliffs, New Jersey: Prentice Hall, 1968.

Blauner, R., Black culture: Myth or reality? In Whitten, N.E., Szwed, J.F. (Eds.), *Afro-American Anthropology*. New York: New York Free Press, ©1970. Quotation used by permission.

Breitman, G., *Malcolm X Speaks*. New York: Grove Press, Inc., 1965.

Carkhuff, R.R., and Pierce, R., Differing effects of therapist race and social class upon patient depth of self exploration in the initial interview. *Journal of Consulting Psychology*, 1967, *31*, 632-634.

Chisholm, S., *Unbought and Unbossed*. New York: Avon Books, 1971.

Cotler, S.B., and Guerra, J., *Assertion Training: A Humanistic-Behavioral Guide to Self-Dignity*. Champaign, Ill.: Research Press, 1976.

DuBois, W.E.B., *Autobiography of W.E.B. DuBois*. New York: International Publishers, 1968.

DuBois, W.E.B., *The Souls of Black Folk*. New York: Fawcett, 1961.

Ellison, R., *Invisible Man*. New York: Random House, Inc., 1952.

Fanon, F.B., *Black Skin, White Masks*. New York: Grove Press, 1967.

Fensterheim, H., and Baer, J., *Don't Say Yes When You Want To Say No*. New York: Dell, 1975.

Gordon, T., White and black psychology. *Journal of Social Issues,* 1973, *29,* 88-89.

Gordonne, C., Quoted in *Newsweek,* May 25, 1970, 95.

Grier, W.H., and Cobbs, P.M., *Black Rage.* New York: Basic Books, 1968.

Grier, W.H., and Cobbs, P.M., *The Jesus Bag.* New York: McGraw-Hill, 1971.

Hare, N., *The Black Anglo-Saxons.* N.Y.: Collier (Macmillan), 1970.

Harper, F.D., and Stone, W.O., Toward a theory of transcendent counseling with blacks. *Journal of Non-White Concerns,* 1974, 193-194.

Haskins, J., and Butts, H.F., *The Psychology of Black Language.* New York: Barnes and Noble, 1973.

Hayes, W.A., and Banks, W.M., The nigger box or a redefinition of a counselor's role. In Jones, R.L. (Ed.), *Black Psychology.* New York: Harper & Row, 1972.

Hill, H., Blacks still lag in jobs, income. "Opinion," *The Los Angeles Times* March 7, 1976. Quotation used by permission.

Hoagland, E., Essence of motherfucker. *The Journal of Black Poetry.* Summer, 1971.

Hoagland, E., *Black Velvet.* Self-published at the Claremont Colleges, 1970.

Jones, R., The black psychologist as consultant and therapist. In Jones, R.L. (Ed.), *Black Psychology.* New York: Harper & Row, 1972.

Jones, L., *The Dutchman.* New York: Morrow, 1964.

Jones, L., *Black Psychology.* New York: Harper & Row, 1972.

Jourard, S., and Laskow, L., Some factors in self disclosure. *Journal of Abnormal Psychology,* 1958, *56,* 91-98.

Killens, J.O., *Black Man's Burden.* New York: Pocket Books, 1969.

Lazarus, A.A., *Behavior Therapy and Beyond.* New York: McGraw-Hill, 1971.

Lazarus, A.A., and Fay, A., *I Can If I Want To.* New York: William Morrow and Company, 1975.

Ledvinka, J.D., Race of the employment interviewer and the language elaboration of black job seekers. Unpublished doctoral dissertation. University of Michigan, 1969.

Lester, J., *Look Out Whitey, Black Power's Gon Get Your Mama!* New York: Grove Press, 1968.

Little, M., (See X, Malcolm).

Litwack, L., *North of Slavery: The Negro in the Free States, 1790-1860.* Chicago: University of Chicago Press, 1961.

McCord, A., and Willie, C., *Black Students at White Colleges.* New York: Praeger, 1972.

McGwine, B., Black visions, white realities. *Change,* 1972, *3* (3), 28-34.

Nobles, W., Psychological research and the black self-concept: A critical review. *Journal of Social Issues,* 1973, *29* (1), 11-31.

Phelps, S., and Austin, N., *The Assertive Woman.* San Luis Obispo, California: Impact Publishers, Inc., 1975.

Salter, A., *Conditioned Reflex Therapy.* New York: Farrar, Strauss, and Gireaux, 1949.

Stalvey, L.M., *Getting Ready – The Education of a White Family in Inner City Schools.* New York: William Morrow and Company, 1974.

Stampp, K.M., *The Peculiar Institution – Slavery in the Ante-Bellum South.* New York: Random House, 1956.

Stikes, S.C., A conceptual map of black student development problems. *Journal of Non-White Concerns,* 1975 (October), 26.

Takaki, R., The black child savage in ante-bellum America. In Nash, G.B., and Weiss, R. (Eds.), *The Great Fear: Race in the Mind of America.* New York: Holt, Rinehart and Winston, Inc., 1970.

Thomas, C.W., *Boys No More.* Beverly Hills, California: Glencoe Press, 1971.

Thomas, C.W., The system-maintenance role of white psychologist. *Journal of Social Issues,* 1973, *29* (1), 57-65.

Whitten, N.E., and Szwed, J.F., *Afro-American Anthropology.* New York: New York Free Press, 1970.

Wilcox, R.C., (Ed.), *The Psychological Consequences of Being a Black American.* New York: John Wiley and Sons, 1971.

Wolkan, G.H., Moriwaki, S., and Williams, K.J., Race and social class as factors in the orientation toward psychotherapy. *Journal of Counseling Psychology,* 1973, *20,* 312-316.

Wolpe, J., *The Practice of Behavior Therapy.* New York: Pergamon Press, ©1969 (2nd ed., 1973). Quotation used by permission.

Woodward, C.V., *The Strange Career of Jim Crow.* New York: Oxford University Press, Third Edition, 1974.

Wright, R., *Black Boy.* New York: Harper & Row, 1945.

X, Malcolm, (with Haley, A.), *The Autobiography of Malcolm X.* New York: Grove Press, 1965.

APPENDIX I

As pointed out in Chapter VI, Black Rappin and Cappin, white puzzlement at black language can easily turn to being offended, angered or frightened. Indeed, the author and publishers recognize that some readers will react in these ways to the following material. Nevertheless, the message is of such key importance to the concept of the subtleties of black language and its effect upon whites, that we have elected to present this fuller treatment.

The idea that a most offensive word (to whites) has great poetic variety is conveyed in the work of my friend Everett Hoagland, printed below:

Essence of Motherfucker

listen motherfucker!

polio is a bitch but
cancer is a motherfucker
a red-neck is a bastard but
an uncle tom is a motherfucker
the ghetto is fucked but
apartheid is a motherfucker
hard work in hot weather
is a motherfucker
siberia is as cold as a motherfucker
and death
is an absolute motherfucker

john henry was definitely
a cock-strong motherfucker
a "Mark III" (or an "El De")
is a pretty motherfucker
the moon shot was a bold motherfucker
a black womans' good lovin'
is a sweet and thorough motherfucker
and our music, without question,
is a world reknown motherfucker

in life
you're either a good motherfucker or
a bad motherfucker

a together brother
is a boss motherfucker
and sisters say
a good man
is a b-a-d motherfucker
however
a **bad** motherfucker
is never a rotten motherfucker
because a **bad** motherfucker
is basically
a good motherfucker

obviously
the word motherfucker
is a motherfucker

This poem was originally intended for inclusion in Hoagland's
first book, *Black Velvet* (1970) but withheld because of concerns for
white reactions at the time of publication. It was first published in *The
Journal of Black Poetry*, Summer 1971, Copyright © 1971 by Everett
Hoagland, and used by permission of Everett Hoagland.

● ● ●

The discussion of the word in Andrews and Owens *Black Language* point out that the specific white definition of sexual incest is
only one of the intended uses of the word among blacks, although
whites generally react to the word on only one level.

MOTHERFUCKER — (also pronounced MOTHAFUCKA)

"It defies definition. You can't express what it means. Anything
before or afterward ain't what it is. Never has, never will be. George
Foreman's a bad MOTHAFUCKA. 'Retha Franklin is a beautiful
MOTHAFUCKA same as Ray Charles is. Now I can call someone a

fucka just like calling him a MOTHAFUCKA and it ain't got nothing to do with fucking anybody's mama. I could be madder 'n hell at the dude or think he's doing as bad as God. As to the slang of MOTHAFUCKA, the white man has always tried to pin what Black people have said into his own frame of reference. That's why he'd describe MOTHAFUCKA as a negative and slang word. Like what the word says, fucking a mother. But that ain't where it is." (Candy — Phoenix House, Harlem) A cat that is so bad (see BAD) that he could get your mama and be in your face tellin' you about it, with nothing you could do about it, is a definite MOTHAFUCKA.

MOTHAFUCKA can be used as a verbal symbol crowned atop the height of beauty, bliss, and soul. In between the high and low meanings of MOTHAFUCKA, the language gives the people license to use MOTHAFUCKA any MOTHAFUCKIN way it comes out of your mouth.

It is used as an intensifier also, and a name for someone, an appelative, like Jack.

Examples of MOTHAFUCKING usages:
1. Anger. "MOTHAFUCKA! What's wrong with you?
2. Greeting. "Waz hapnin', MOTHAFUCKA?"
3. Question. "Say, how much a MOTHAFUCKA are you now?"
4. Declarative statement. "That cat sure is a deep MOTHAFUCKA."
5. Frustration. "How do you get this MOTHAFUCKIN thing done?"
6. Positive force. "We're goin' to get those MOTHAFUCKAS."
7. The unknown. "Where in the MOTHAFUCK are they?"
8. When the power structure, the establishment, is giving you a hard time, then you are being fucked and those who are doing it to you are the MOTHAFUCKAS.

From Andrews, M. and Owens, P.T., *Black Language*. Los Angeles: Seymour-Smith, ©1973. Used by permission of Seymour-Smith Publisher, P.O. Box 25228, Los Angeles, CA 90025.

APPENDIX II

☆**Publisher's Note:** Dr. Cheek's arguments in Chapter V for high risk interventions are persuasive. Nevertheless, facilitators should be aware that to begin at the level of highest inhibition, while getting at "the problem target" quickly and directly, may induce such a high anxiety level as to lessen the chances of successful assertion. If this approach is used, we believe the client should be informed of the risks of failure, and encouraged not to give up if assertion is not immediately successful. Salter and others suggest a gradual approach, starting with less risky situations and thereby building a foundation of success before attempting more difficult assertions.